Project Me

for busy mothers

Project Me

for busy mothers

A practical guide to finding a happier balance

KELLY PIETRANGELI

First published in Great Britain in 2018 by Orion Spring
an imprint of The Orion Publishing Group Ltd
Carmelite House, 50 Victoria Embankment
London EC4Y 0DZ

An Hachette UK Company

1 3 5 7 9 10 8 6 4 2

Design: Kelly Pietrangeli, Basia Taboda & Briony Hartley

A CIP catalogue record for this book is
available from the British Library.

ISBN: 978 1 4091 7025 9

Printed in Great Britain by
CPI Group (UK) Ltd, Croydon, CR0 4YY

www.orionbooks.co.uk

ORION
SPRING

For my dear friends and
amazing Power Pals,
Anna and Suzie
'Just ASK'

Contents

Introduction

Do the demands of motherhood tip you out of balance, leaving some parts of your life brushed aside? Are you pulled in all directions – never sure if anything you're doing is 'good enough'?

Most of us are so busy reacting to events in our lives that we don't pause to examine what's working and what's not. It's easy to lose the plot on the bigger-picture stuff when there's always **so** much that needs attention.

You may not realise you're neglecting yourself, even when you're frazzled and short-fused. You don't notice that your relationship needs more attention, until you start drifting apart. Without enough fun, friends or hobbies, you can get into a total rut. Take your eye off the ball with finances, organising or cleaning and suddenly you're in a deep mess.

This book is designed to help you step off that crazy hamster wheel, catch your breath and gain some fresh perspective. You'll start giving yourself more credit for what **is** going well and fully appreciate all of the good in your life. You'll become a pro problem solver who figures things out and moves forward. There'll be no stopping you once you get off the starting blocks.

How do I know this is possible? Because several years ago **I was in your shoes**. Fed up, exasperated and desperate for a better way.

I hit a real low point when my kids were starting school. I assumed things would get easier once I was out of the physically exhausting, sleep-deprived early days, yet as they grew older, whole new challenges took over.

I finally stopped hoping things would get better on their own and started getting proactive. It took some time and figuring out, but I managed to pull my act together, one small step at a time, by creating my Project Me.

My life now flows with a lot more ease. I've lost that perpetually overwhelmed feeling and I get more done with less effort. I've discovered my passions and a sense of purpose that makes me happy to begin each new day. My little pipsqueaks have grown into taller-than-me teenagers and I'm incredibly proud of them – and me – for how far we've come after such a shaky start.

I'm here to show you some great shortcuts to speed you into a better place in much less time than it took me.

I'm not called the Mama Motivator for nothing!

Becoming the expert of you

As you read this book you'll see that getting my act together has been a process. And I still don't always have my act together!

It's taken me a lot of trial and error over the years to figure out what works best for me and for my family. What I'm offering you are tools and inspiration to create your own Project Me so you can become the expert of you and your family. You are uniquely different from me, your best friend, your sister, your mother and every woman on this planet. There is no cookie-cutter template of how you should manage your life – and that's a good thing! Your beautiful life is yours to paint in any colours and style you can dream of. Let go of your limitations, seize the wheel and drive yourself towards a happier life – enjoying all of the amazing scenery along the way.

Taking better control of your life doesn't mean being a control freak. Nor is it about perfection. It's about freeing yourself up to enjoy the journey.

I'm here as your co-pilot, helping you keep your eyes on the road and giving you a simple map to guide you along. I promise: I'm good company, we'll have a lot of laughs and I'll make sure you don't drive off any cliffs.

So if we're doing this road trip together, you'll want to get to know me a little better . . .

Who is Kelly P. from Project Me?

I spent the first half of my life in America and the second half in England, making me a kind of a Yank-Brit hybrid. One of my kids calls me 'mum'; the other calls me 'mom'.

I've worked in a string of ridiculously fun jobs in Hollywood, including being Johnny Depp's press assistant, and then making music videos. I moved to London when I was twenty-four and became a record cover designer.

In my late twenties I met the guy of my dreams, got married, and used the fringe benefits of my job in the music industry to go to free concerts and parties several nights a week. Life was super fun! It was all going fairy-tale dreamy until . . .

Cue sound of screeching needle dragging across record

We decided to have a baby.

It would be easy. Babies sleep a lot, right? I'd leave my job and set up at home as a freelance graphic designer, working as my little darling snoozed. But, after my smooth-sailing pregnancy, my son's birth was traumatic. I hadn't properly addressed my deep fear of childbirth and how that fear would affect the delivery.

Things didn't get much easier back at home. Breastfeeding was an agony I endured with gritted teeth, bleeding nipples and double mastitis, all while sitting on an inflatable doughnut feeling miserable. Sleep deprivation is an evil thing. I'd always been an eight-hours-a-night kinda gal. Now my mind and body felt like they were turning against me.

I felt weepy, ugly and frumpy, and I completely lost my sex drive for a long time after the birth. Some essential part of my being felt lost and life was now about trying to muddle through, one day at a time. The thought of being responsible for this child for the next eighteen years threw me into complete overwhelm.

I loved my son deeply and his smile brought me immense rushes of joy. I adored being his mother, even if I didn't like many of the side effects that came with it – including a chronic case of *I'm-not-doing-anything-good-enough* syndrome. Maybe you've suffered from that one yourself?

For one whole year, I lived without goals of my own. I had goals for my son: getting him to sleep through the night, weaning him, taking his first steps; but none of those things was for *me*.

Reading my journal entries takes me straight back to that discouraging period of my life. Perhaps you can relate to how I was feeling:

Lack of energy. Disorganised. Overwhelmed with constant lists of things to do that never get done. Procrastination. Guilt. Bored and frustrated. Complete loss of libido. No creativity or motivation.

In one journal entry I had a bit of a breakthrough:

I need to create more 'me time' for self-reflection, goal setting, inspirational reading, and clearing my mind. I waste too much time watching TV. Unless something really watchable is on, do something else. Create time for lovemaking, don't expect it to just happen. Pamper myself. Burn candles. Create a calm environment. Play chill-out music when cooking. Make our home a sanctuary.

I wrote that my intention for the year ahead was **to create a healthy balance by giving more energy to the most important things and people in my life**.

And so, my friend, the seed of Project Me was planted. And it's been growing like a wildflower ever since!

Becoming the Project Manager of my life

It all began with an idea to use a ring binder folder with colour-coded tabbed sections for each area of my life. I loaded it up with blank, lined paper as if I was all ready for some kind of hugely important project. I had no idea what I was doing, but I felt excited about it anyway.

I figured it was like managing a house renovation with separate sections for plumbing, electricity, interior design and outdoor landscaping. My life needed sorting out in **all** areas, so I broke it down into Love, Family, Health, Personal Growth, Fun, Money, Work and Productivity. Having it all in one place helped me become the Project Manager of my life. I used my folder to start collecting ideas for how to build my dream life. Once I got organised, things began to improve quickly.

In 2011 I was asked to write a motivational column for a friend's lifestyle website, which renewed my love of writing. In 2013 I launched the Project Me blog, sharing personal stories of the challenges I'd overcome in all areas of my life. I was amazed that within three months over 1,000 mothers had signed up to the weekly Project Me newsletter. Emails began pouring in to say how much they appreciated my honest stories and practical strategies which they were implementing for themselves.

A global movement

Fast forward to today: Project Me has morphed into something beyond my wildest dreams. I now run online courses, workshops and retreats, and work with women individually. Mothers all over the world are creating their own versions of Project Me, sharing their wins and inspiring others to join in. (Mama Power – woo hoo!) Kids are like little sponges – soaking up the vibes that their happy mamas are giving out. It puts a smile on my face to think about the positive effect Project Me is having on future generations.

You're about to learn how to treat your own life like an exciting, ongoing project. Once you get going, you'll know what it's like to be less reactive and more **pro**active. You'll realise that *you* are in control of your own happiness and you'll pour more energy into creating a life you love.

It's not selfish to put the focus on you

Many mothers suffer from guilt, especially when it comes to doing something for themselves. They'll organise everything they think their child needs – buying them more things, chauffeuring them from one activity to another – yet they'd never consider spending that kind of time or money on themselves. Eventually this kind of self-sacrifice leads to frustration, stress, exhaustion and resentment.

If there's a voice in your head telling you that it's selfish to focus on yourself, here's my mini pep talk: it's better for your child when you're happy and you look after yourself. It'll give you more energy to give them and make you calmer and more fun to be around. Imagine what a great role model you'll be for them. If not for you, do it for them.

Losing yourself to motherhood

If you're still deep in the baby and toddler trenches, it may feel all-consuming and never-ending. It certainly did for me! Gently remind yourself that it's only a stage. The more you stay connected to yourself now, the easier it'll be to live a well-balanced life and not lose yourself completely to motherhood. Do whatever you can in a slow, consistent way and don't be too hard on yourself or wish away these early days. Let go of perfection and go with the flow as often as you can.

If you feel like you've already lost who you were before becoming a mother, Project Me will help you to find her again, as it did for Lauren and Julie:

> I'd completely lost my voice. I had no idea who I was as a person. The Project Me Life Wheel was the first tool that actually helped me organise my thoughts and my fears in a way that was empowering rather than overwhelming. It helped me pick one thing to focus on improving. Once a month I do a check-in with the Project Me Life Wheel so I won't get so anxious again.
> **–Lauren**

> I came across Project Me at a time when I was a bit overwhelmed with life. The Project Me Life Wheel helped me to identify the areas where I needed to take action and prompted me to think through some baby steps I could take to get where I wanted to be. I've made more time for me, become more mindful and am taking better care of myself. My friends and family have noticed the difference in me and overwhelm happens much less often these days. When I feel it coming on I know I have the Project Me tools I need to help me through it.
> **–Julie**

I
create
a life
I
love.

#ProjectMe

Prepare for Success! Three Tips for Making This Book Work for You

This isn't the kind of book you read once, then put on the shelf. Your life is ever-evolving and the strategies you'll learn can be applied over and over at different stages. Here's how to navigate your way through it with the greatest success.

Success Tip #1: Don't just read about – DO IT!

Use the **Take Action!** call-outs and the **Project Me Action Sheets** to *write it down and make it happen*. Printable versions of all Action Sheets in this book are also located in a special section on the Project Me website, where you can grab them over and over again as needed. Bookmark this page for easy access: www.myprojectme.com/action-sheets.

Throughout the book you'll find **Journal Prompts**. If you haven't kept a journal since you were an angst-ridden teenager, this is nothing to fear. Something magical happens when you put a pen to paper. When you identity whatever is causing stress, worry, anxiety, anger, sadness or frustration in your life, it gives you the opportunity to explore it and find solutions. Any notebook will do, but I wish I'd started a nice new journal when I began my Project Me. *Just saying.*

To help you realise that you're not alone in your struggles, I've shared my own personal stories, as well as accounts from some of the many mothers I've worked with and who've taken part in my Project Me surveys. I hope these will further inspire you to take action.

Becoming the expert of you also means doing some 'me-search'. Don't miss my **Treasure Trove of Tried and Tested Resources** at the back of the book. These are divided into your 8 Key Life Areas (corresponding to the book's 8 chapters) and include books, websites, apps and podcasts that'll help you take things further.

Success Tip #2: Read it your way

There are a couple of ways you could approach this book, depending on your personality type or even your mood today.

Option A: Start with the Project Me Life Wheel® exercise coming up next. Identify which of your 8 Key Life Areas you want to focus on first, then head to that chapter for inspiration to get started.

Highly recommended if you want to follow more of a step-by-step formula for making positive changes in your life.

Option B: Feel your way around the book. Read the table of contents, see what's calling to you at the moment and head there. I'm also a fan of closing your eyes, asking the book to give you what you need right now, then opening it up to any page and soaking up the message.

Good if you prefer to go off-piste and find your own way.

Success Tip #3: Plan a regular Hot Date With Yourself

Once a month, schedule in a date with yourself to do a Project Me Life Wheel® review, using your journal and Action Sheets to get clear about what needs doing. This flags up problems before they turn into full-blown issues. Getting to know yourself better and planning and figuring things out on paper are valuable uses of your time. The investment will pay off in ways you can't even imagine right now.

Maybe you're thinking, 'But I don't have enough time.' 'I won't be able to do this properly.' 'This will be great after I _____.' (Fill in the blank with whatever you think has to happen before you can get started.)

Don't wait for a magical opening to appear in your life. It won't happen. **'Prioritise' means 'to choose something over something else'.** That means something else has to give, at least a little, so you can prioritise your Project Me.

If you've scheduled a Hot Date With Yourself, set a 'no excuses' rule. When the time comes and you're inevitably busy, tired, stressed or lack motivation – stick to your rule. Don't let fluctuating moods affect your commitment to making yourself a priority. Once you get started you'll be happy you did.

If you genuinely feel like you don't have an hour out of a 720-hour month to sit down with your Project Me, then it's probably a good idea to start with the Productivity chapter (page 63). Once you get some systems and strategies in place, it'll free you up to take better control of your waking hours. Whatever small, baby steps you take towards making your life run more smoothly, the happier you'll feel.

Are you ready to take hold of the wheel? Come on, let's go!

The Project Me Life Wheel®

When I work with mothers, no matter what stage they're at, I always encourage them to step back and look at their life objectively. What's going well? What could be better? What needs some focus **now**?

What can feel like your big, fat, messy life may actually boil down to some issues in one or two areas that can be improved quite easily once you put your mind to them. By separating your life into 8 Key Life Areas, you'll get a better perspective about what's making you feel stressed, anxious, unhappy or unfulfilled – then you can **do** something about it.

Based on a popular life coaching exercise, I've reinvented the life wheel – giving it the Project Me spin to include life areas specifically relevant to busy mothers like us.

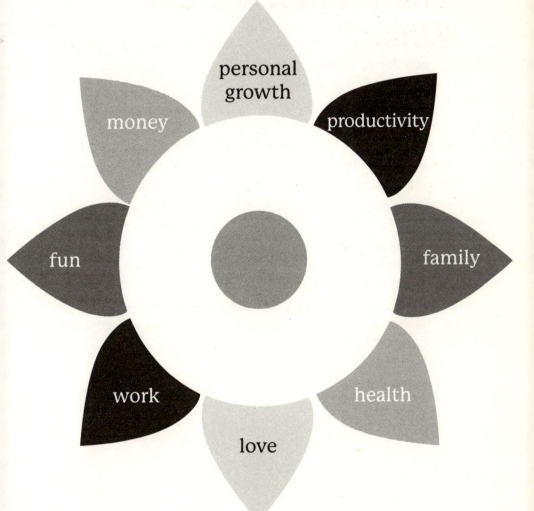

The Project Me Life Wheel® gives you an objective bird's-eye view of your life to help you see where you're currently out of balance. Balance is not about giving the same amount of energy to **all** areas of your life simultaneously. It's about being *aware* of what needs your focus at any given time and recognising the symptoms of feeling **out** of balance before things get out of hand.

Here are some emotional side effects you might experience on a regular basis when your life is out of whack.

How many of these can you relate to?

Overwhelmed	Rushed	Discouraged
Stressed	Dissatisfied	Insecure
Anxious	Grumpy	Unmotivated
Worried	Resentful	Uninspired
Guilty	Bored	Unfulfilled

Plus physical effects, such as:

Exhaustion	Weak immune system	Disrupted digestion
Poor health	Low energy	Loss of libido
Pain	Weight gain or loss	Bad skin

Feeling 'in balance' doesn't mean that all of life is flowing perfectly and you never have any of these negative emotional or physical side effects. It's about having an overall sense of what's going well and what could use some extra focus. When you have a balanced sense of objectivity over your life, you see challenges as 'figure-out-able'. You also give yourself credit and appreciate what *is* going smoothly. We don't do this last part often enough!

You may find you've become overly child-centric since becoming a mother. Your whole world might feel like it revolves around your family. Maybe you've forgotten how to make yourself happy. The Life Wheel offers a different perspective: a life in which **you** are in the centre and eight important areas bloom around you. **You are a mother – and so much more.**

Driving instructions for the Project Me Life Wheel®

You've heard me talk about it long enough – it's time to get started!

Read through each of the 8 Key Life Area prompts on the following pages. This will get your thoughts flowing about how each area of your life is going right now. Using a pencil, circle a number on the Life Wheel from 1–10. A lower score indicates a need for improvement. A higher score means it's going well. A ten doesn't mean it's 'perfect' – perfection is unachievable and crazy-making! A ten simply means that it's going very well and doesn't need any specific focus right now.

Be kind to yourself. If you're in a bad mood you might feel like marking yourself super low in everything. A score of one or two is reserved for crisis situations, so remain objective and fair in your self-assessment. This is a tool to help you see where you're currently out of balance and what could use some focused attention right now.

If you don't want to write directly in the book, enter your email address at www.myprojectme.com and the Project Me Life Wheel® will be sent to you to print out and use again and again. Write today's date on it and print a fresh one each month to observe the natural ups and downs as well as any areas where you're repeatedly stuck.

You can also write your scores on a piece of paper. *There's no excuse not to start today.*

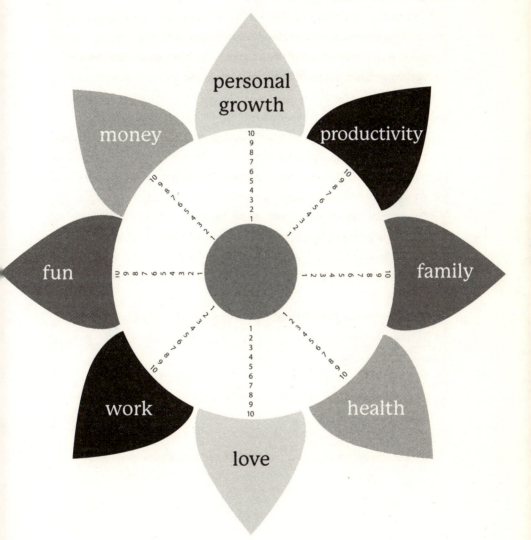

Personal growth

Getting to know and understand yourself better is the key to being the best version of yourself. Life is easier to navigate when you have a healthy mindset and understand your emotions.

How's your mindset? Are you a worrier? A perfectionist? A control freak?

Does your inner voice speak nicely to you? Do you beat yourself up or put yourself down too often?

Is your brain like a runaway train? Do you overthink things? Find it hard to shut off the mental chatter?

Do you know what your emotions and moods are telling you?

Do you get enough time for yourself, or do you put everyone and everything else first?

Would you like to meditate regularly? Do yoga? Journal? Read inspiring books?

Do you have clear goals? Do you know what you want from life and what makes you happy?

If you feel very inspired and fulfilled, mark yourself accordingly. If not, give yourself a lower score. There are many small things you can do to enhance this part of your life once you put your mind to it.

Productivity

This is everything to do with organisation, time management and running the show! When you feel on top of your busy-ness, you create more energy and space for the things and people you love.

Do you feel like a headless chicken? Never enough hours in the day?

Does your to-do list feel never-ending?

Are you clear about your priorities, or do you do whatever's in front of your face each day?

Could you use some systems and strategies for managing your time and energy better?

Are you feeling overwhelmed? Is there too much going on at once?

Are you procrastinator? Do you find it hard to say 'no'?

Are you a meal planner or do you wing it with food shopping and cooking?

Does your house need better organisation/de-cluttering?

Do you get the help you need, or do you feel like you're doing everything yourself?

If this is a low-score area for you, you're not alone. Time management and organisation is a challenging area, but some focus and an action plan will get you sorted. Honestly!

Family

Think of your child/children, any brothers or sisters, parents/in-laws or step-parents and other extended family. No need to include your partner here, as there's a separate section for your love life later.

Does your child need some particular help or support right now?

Would you like to be more patient, shout less or listen better?

Are you confident with your parenting skills? Do you have strategies to deal with issues?

Do you give your energy to what's going wrong, or do you actively look for and acknowledge the good?

Would you like to build a closer connection? Improve communication? Tame technology?

If you have more than one child, do you give each one the individual attention they need?

Do sibling squabbles drive you nuts?

Does anything with your extended family need figuring out?

Investing time and energy in your family life now pays off in the long term and saves future problems from developing. How would you score this area of your life right now? Does it need more focus or is it going well?

Health and Wellbeing

This section covers everything from a healthy body to a healthy mind. If you're suffering poor health, it affects all other areas of your life too.

Do you make looking after your health a priority or does it drop to the bottom of the list?

Are you up to date on your screenings and tests (smear, mammogram, mole checks)?

Could you make your meals more nutritious? Do you drink enough water?

Do you lack time or motivation to get enough exercise? Need to find your fitness groove?

Are your energy levels buzzing or flagging? Could you use some energy boosters?

Do you recognise the symptoms of stress, or has it become your 'new normal'?

Are you breathing deeply and fully – or just the minimum to survive?

Are you sleep-deprived? Is it self-induced by getting to bed too late?

Do you suffer from depression? Are you managing a chronic illness?

Would you welcome some tools to help you keep a healthy mind, such as mindfulness or meditation?

Be honest (no beating yourself up allowed here!) and mark where you are right now. A lower score means that it's a focus area for you.

Love

Whether you're in a relationship or flying solo, this is an opportunity to look at your love life and whether it needs some preventive care or troubleshooting.

Is marriage maintenance a priority for you? For your partner?

Do you have enough 'we' time?

How's your communication and connection lately?

Do you fight fair? Make up easily after an argument?

Is your sex life hot . . . or not?

Stuck in a rut? Worried you might be drifting apart?

Are you pondering separation or going through a divorce?

If you're single, are you ready to find love again?

Sometimes it's easy to get too comfortable and stop making an effort in your relationship. Even if things are going well right now, take steps to keep it that way. Deal with issues or problems as they arise rather than letting them fester and grow. Listen to your heart and give your love life a score.

Work

If you're feeling conflicted, either because you do or don't work, this section helps you to look at things more objectively. This is also the place to mark your satisfaction if you volunteer, are active at school or on a committee.

Are you on maternity leave and debating about going back to work?
Concerned about an upcoming return to your job, or starting a whole
  new one?
Feeling guilty for working? Or frustrated about not working?
Do you feel bored or unfulfilled as a stay-at-home mother?
Do you have a support network? Are you getting the help you need?
Would you like to find work that fits around your family?
Are you thinking about starting your own business?
Would you like to explore volunteer opportunities?

If work isn't an area of focus for you right now, mark it as a ten and move on.
If not, score it on how important it feels to your life right now.

Fun

This area's about fun, friendships, social life, cultural fixes, hobbies and interests. It often gets overlooked at the expense of everything else that needs to be fitted in. Without fun life's got no juice!

Have you forgotten what fun feels like lately?

Could you use some ideas for how to inject more fun into your life?

Would you like to understand yourself better socially on the introvert-extrovert scale?

Are you seeing enough of your friends? Do you need to reach out more and initiate plans?

Do you find it hard to make new friends? Lack meaningful friendships?

Are there any specific friendship issues that are dragging you down?

Are you having enough fun together as a family?

Would it feel good to learn something new, get your cogs turning and feel inspired again?

How's your fun-o-meter looking right now? Full to bursting or pretty lame?

If you need to step up the fun quota, mark yourself lower to motivate you to do something about it.

Money

All things financial are included in this area, including wills and important documents. It's also an opportunity to dive into your money mindset and identify any blocks to the flow of abundance in your life.

Do you have money worries that are niggling away at you or keeping you up at night?

How do you feel about money? Does financial abundance flow freely, or could you be blocking it by having a scarcity/lack mindset?

Are you in charge of the money system and wish you had a little help? Or do you turn a blind eye?

Are you and your partner able to talk about money openly?

Do you spend money mindfully or do you get caught up in consumerism or comparison traps?

Do you want to create a strategy for saving, budgeting and tracking your expenditures?

Are gratitude, charity and giving important to you? If so, are you living by those values?

Do you need to make or update your will? Do you know where to find key financial documents – insurance policies, tax returns, household bills, wills?

No real concerns around any of this right now? Give yourself a high score – otherwise circle the number that feels right.

Time to connect the dots!

Plot each score on your wheel and then join them up to make a circle, as in this example. How wonky is your wheel?

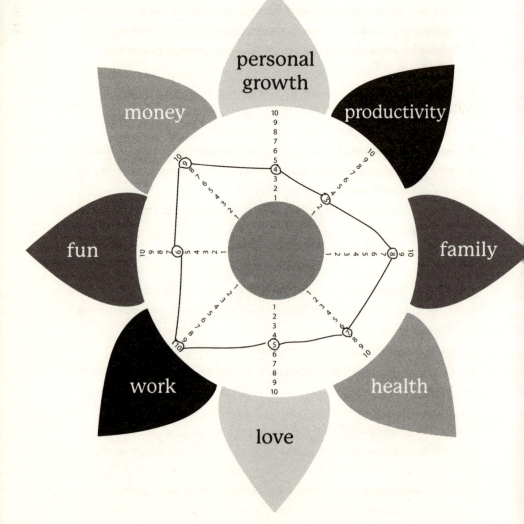

Is it all zig-zagged and crazy-looking? If it were an actual wheel would it turn smoothly or would you be crashing into a ditch? Don't worry if your circle's on the small side or not particularly round. Your Life Wheel helps you see more clearly where to take action so you can make positive changes.

It's also a great opportunity to recognise the parts of your life that *are* flowing smoothly. We tend to focus too much on what's *not* working and don't give ourselves nearly enough credit for what's going well. You're doing better than you think!

Doing this exercise every month will show you that fluctuating scores are a natural part of life. Over time it will also flag up areas that are repeatedly low so you can do something about it. Date and keep each completed wheel in a Project Me folder. These will be your key insight into how your life is flowing in the bigger scheme of things.

What now?

It's really tempting to want to dive in and make everything a higher score straight away, but best results come when you slow down and focus on getting one area of your life into a better place. When you scatter your efforts, you get overwhelmed – and then paralysis kicks in and you do nothing. It's far better to **start small and take baby steps**.

Look at your Life Wheel scores and ask yourself these questions:

1. Which one life area might be having a negative knock-on effect on other areas too?
2. If I took some small steps in one area, could I automatically improve the rest of my life too?
3. What feels too hard and overwhelming to start with right now?
4. What could I begin with that feels doable so I can feel a sense of achievement before tackling something bigger?

There is no right or wrong place to start.

Some life areas are admittedly easier to get moving on with great gusto than others. It's a lot less scary to work on your time management than your relationship. It's more nerve-wracking to think about finding a new job than clearing out your closet.

Here's a choice you can make right now, and either option is perfectly fine:

Option A: Feel the fear/discomfort and do it anyway.
This means choosing a challenging area, being brave and taking those first few steps to improve things.

Option B: Choose a different life area that also needs focus, but feels easier right now. Honestly, that's OK too. When you feel success in one area it'll build your confidence.

Here's what other mothers have said about using the Project Me Life Wheel®:

> I was in a bad place when I found Project Me. I had lost sight of me and my whole life felt out of control. It was scary to work through the questions on the Life Wheel. I felt uncomfortable and challenged, everything scored low and I felt overwhelmed for a few days, but I kept going and began feeling so much transformation and hope. I realised I needed to take control, and to have the strength to do this I needed to restore my perception of myself, and to stop procrastinating and do something. I keep all my old Life Wheels and only compare them once I've rescored. It's now so fun to see how much progress I've made. You helped me find a wiser, happier, productive me.
>
> **–Sam**

> As I completed/ranked each area of my life on the wheel, I was surprised to see how out of balance I was in some areas. It became so visually obvious once I connected all of the dots and I also saw how interrelated everything is. I realised that by starting with the area that ranked the lowest, I would feel the biggest sense of accomplishment and start to feel more balanced because that was what was throwing the whole thing off!
>
> **–Carrie**

I often feel completely overwhelmed by multiple areas of my life and I like that you suggest to focus on one zone. Has helped me gain some direction in my crazy, working, single-mum life.

—Jill

I was on maternity leave when I did the Life Wheel, and it helped me figure out my direction for my year off. I felt I'd lost part of my identity and this helped me shape the year I wanted to have.

—Joanne

The Project Me Life Wheel is a fantastic tool. Sometimes the results surprise me. Once it showed Work as a 7 or 8, when I'd been feeling it was down in the 1 or 2 area! I think it's about taking a step back and looking at the bigger picture. It helps me so much to get things into perspective and decide where I need to focus next.

—Julia

I do the Life Wheel regularly and encourage my girlfriends to do the same. A couple of years back when I saw that my Work area was very low (stay-at-home mom) I made the decision to get my Master's in Education. I graduated in May and am now working with English Language learners. I am so very fulfilled helping and empowering my students.

—Lisa

Two more Action Sheets

The following **Ideas Into Action** and **Challenge Solver** templates are the two main Action Sheets referred to in every chapter. Printable copies are available at www.myprojectme.com/action-sheets. If you haven't got a printer, use a notebook to capture your thoughts.

IDEAS INTO ACTION

If you're a non-fiction junkie like me, you've probably got books filled with sticky notes, highlighted text and dog-eared pages. All of those 'aha!' and 'I must try that!' ideas are great, but then you close the book, life gets busy and you forget all about them.

I created an Ideas Into Action worksheet to help you capture any juicy ideas you get while reading this book so you'll take action on them. Out of your head, onto paper and into your life!

CHALLENGE SOLVER

Figuring stuff out on paper is always better than churning it around in your head – or pushing it aside, where it gnaws away at you. The answers flow once you **write it down**. The Challenge Solver Action Sheet is a great tool to help you clarify the situation and prompt you to brainstorm some potential solutions. Give it a try and see for yourself!

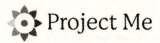 Project Me

Date ..../........../..........

★ Ideas Into Action ★

Life Area _____   Idea

Actions

1. _____

2. _____

3. _____

Life Area _____   Idea

Actions

1. _____

2. _____

3. _____

Life Area _____   Idea

Actions

1. _____

2. _____

3. _____

WWW.MYPROJECTME.COM

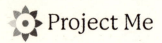
Project Me

Date .... / .... / ....

★ Challenge Solver ★

What's my problem or challenge?

How is this making me feel? What's this problem costing me?

How will I feel to have this solved?

What will happen if I don't take action? How will I feel if I do NOTHING?

What ideas do I have? (What has worked before? What hasn't worked? What could be done differently?)

From your ideas list, choose something to try. What will you do? Get specific. How long will it take? (Often it's less time that you think.) When will you do it? Schedule it in. This is crucial.

If this challenge feels overwhelming, turn the page over and break it down into small manageable chunks. One small step at a time will get you there! CREATE A WRITTEN ACTION PLAN!

WWW.MYPROJECTME.COM

you've got this!

The rest of this book is divided into your 8 Key Life Areas. In each section I've shared some personal experiences of how I've overcome particular obstacles. You may relate to some of my struggles, or maybe they'll get you thinking more clearly about your own. You may feel inspired to try what worked for me, or it may spark ideas for yourself.

I'm not the guru with all of the solutions to your problems, but I am here to offer you hope, inspiration, resources and tools so you can find your own answers.

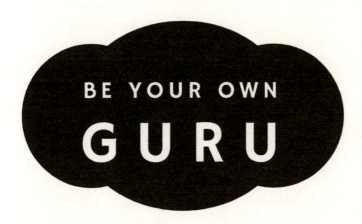

BE YOUR OWN
GURU

personal
growth

Personal Growth

Personal Growth is one petal on the Life Wheel, yet all of Project Me centres around your personal development. It's easier to navigate life when you understand yourself better. You're a much more peaceful and loving mother when your soul is being fed. You'll feel less hard done by, take care of yourself more, eat and sleep better, and see life beyond the laundry pile. You'll have more to give and feel more like that version of yourself that you enjoy being around.

Focusing on your self-development is far from selfish. When you transform yourself, you transform the world around you including, of course, your immediate family. We've all heard the saying, 'If Mama's happy, everybody's happy!' and this is certainly true from my perspective. Just ask my family!

It's normal to flit back and forth between your 'best version' (the one who's patient, calm, kind, relaxed and light-hearted) and your 'poor version' (that other one who's irritable, impatient, snappy, stressed and overwhelmed).

Wouldn't you love to be your best version more often?

That's what this chapter is all about. Finding ways to be less Jekyll and Hyde and more consistently the *you* that you want to be. It's also a chance to explore ways to create a more positive energy for yourself.

Self-Awareness and Mindset

When you operate on autopilot day in and day out without thinking much about *why* you do what you do, think what you think, behave the way you behave, you're missing out on the opportunity to learn and grow. You end up making the same mistakes or getting stuck in a rut.

Your entire approach to life is based on your mindset. Carol Dwek, psychologist and author of *Mindset*, has done some fascinating research to support this. **Fixed-mindset** people are often stubborn about learning new things, feeling as though their current level of understanding is sufficient. They can be sceptical of personal growth or 'self-help' and don't see the point of it. With a sensitivity to being wrong or making a mistake, perfectionism or an all-or-nothing mentality can take over. They may give up (or not even try) if it can't be done 'right'.

Growth-mindset people believe that great personal qualities can be learned, developed or cultivated. They accept feedback, not viewing it as a judgement of their personality, potential or value. A woman with a growth mindset feels eager to boost her knowledge and enjoys exploring, experimenting and stretching herself. She is not as sensitive to criticisms and setbacks don't affect her as badly. She views problems as challenges and looks to solve them.

Your mindset is never totally one type or the other. There are some extreme cases but most of us lie somewhere in between. You can show different mindsets in different situations, depending on what shaped your belief about your particular abilities.

Developing a growth mindset is not only good for you; it's good for your child too. You can model how to use strategies to cope with setbacks and challenges. You'll influence them to be proactive and resourceful.

When I'm struggling with something, I'll admit it to my kids. Rather than painting myself out to be perfect or hiding my problems so as not to burden them, I share what's going on and show them that I'm working on a solution. My efforts are a sign of my strength, not a show of my weaknesses. Now that they're teenagers I can see them displaying the same approach.

Put yourself in a growth mindset as you work on your Project Me by remembering that some days or weeks will be better than others. If you fall off the wagon, climb back on. Forgive yourself for being imperfect. Admit when you're struggling and view setbacks and challenges as solvable.

Your Thoughts Create Your Reality

Imagine your mind as a garden. Positive thoughts are the beautiful flowers that brighten your life. Negative thoughts are the ugly weeds that spread and suffocate the flowers. Tending to your garden is an ongoing process. My natural weed killers are yoga, meditation, inspirational reading and hanging out with positive people. Weed food is worrying about what other people think, taking things personally and stressing out about situations that don't matter or are out of my control. Whenever I catch myself having a drawn-out imaginary conversation ('And if they say this, I'll say that . . .') with absolutely no outcome, I hit my mental pause button, then change the channel by bringing myself back into the present moment.

The way you think determines how you feel emotionally and thus, how you behave. So if you're crabby with your kids, snappy with your spouse, irritable with yourself – it's all created in your own mind. Every morning my son and I say the affirmation, **'As I think, so it is'** as a reminder that our thoughts create our reality.

Below are some common mindset barriers to happiness. As you read each one, think about how frequently you've experienced it in the past week.

- Worrying about the future
- Ruminating over the past
- A need for certainty
- Wanting to control outcomes
- Perfectionism
- Beating yourself up
- Feeling not good enough
- Lack of confidence

- Self-doubt
- Guilt
- Over-concern for what others think about you
- Fear of asking for help
- Putting everyone else first – then resenting it

We all experience these feelings from time to time, but if any of them are steady figures in your day-to-day existence, it has a big impact on your emotions, behaviour and ultimately your entire life.

The good news is that while there are a lot of things in life that are out of your control, it's in your control to take on a more positive mindset. Your self-talk is largely unconscious and automatic, but the more you tune in and notice what that voice in your head is saying, the more you can begin to change it. It just takes practice.

Woven throughout the pages of this book are **Mama Mantras**. These are affirmations which, when repeated to yourself regularly, sink into your subconscious mind until you really start to believe them. Over time you can rewrite any negative beliefs you have about yourself and replace them with positive thoughts and beliefs.

As you notice these Mama Mantras throughout the book, pause and say them to yourself – or share them with your child.

I love and accept myself, exactly as I am

And I love and accept others for who they are.

I give myself credit

I'm doing better than I think.

I am grateful

There is always, always something to
feel grateful for.

Focusing on me
is not selfish

I'm a better mother when
I look after myself.

I drop
the guilt

I'm doing my best with what I've got.

I take one small step at a time

It will get me there faster
than doing nothing.

I can start
over anytime

A bad moment doesn't make me
a bad mama.

I let go of
perfection

It doesn't have to be perfect.
Good enough is good enough today.

Quieting Your Inner Mean Girl

You know that little voice in your head that loves to put you down? The one that tells you that you're not a good enough mother/daughter/partner/friend or that you're stupid/ugly/fat/hopelessly unorganised. (Fill in the blanks with your own rubbish.)

Your inner mean girl fills your head with so much junk that you begin to believe it's true and once that happens, you've got yourself a whole set of **self-limiting beliefs**. They affect the way you think and act every day.

Maybe these beliefs stem from the way your parents or a teacher spoke to you as a child or the way someone else treated you along the way. Rather than pointing the blame and playing the victim, it's time to recognise when that mean inner critic is speaking so you can begin to quiet it.

Telling your inner mean girl to 'shut up' or 'go away' only creates an internal battle. It's far better to simply notice and observe what she's trying to say to you. Is she attempting to protect you from potential embarrassment or failure by telling you not to even try? Is she messing with your mindset and holding you back?

Be light-hearted with your inner mean girl. I love what Tara Mohr suggests in her book *Playing Big*. Give your inner critic a name. (I call mine *Betty*). When you notice your critic trying to put you down or telling you that you can't do something, tell her, 'Thanks, but I've got this covered.' Take back the wheel by reassuring the fearful part of you that things are under control and everything's going to be fine.

Begin to see when self-limiting beliefs are holding you back from trying something new, accomplishing a goal or preventing you from being your best version. If 'Thanks, but I've got this' isn't working, put pen to paper and get to the bottom of it. Remember, Project Me is about taking good ideas and putting them into action.

Journal Prompt

Start a page called My Self-Limiting Beliefs to identify the beliefs and stories that may be holding you back.

I am not good enough at _____

I am afraid to try _____

I am not ready for _____

I don't deserve _____

_____ prevents me from making changes in my life.

What excuses do I use?

What else holds me back?

You may come up with a whole list straight away, or you might start hearing them in your head over the next days and weeks. As you notice one, add it to the list.

Now question these beliefs by asking yourself:

★ How do I know this is absolutely true?

★ Where's the proof?

★ How is this belief limiting me?

★ How could I prove it wrong?

★ What's my mean inner critic trying to protect me from? Embarrassment/failure/hurt?

Give your critic a name and tell her, 'Thanks, _____, but I've got this.'

You Choose Your Feelings

Here's a cold hard truth: no one can *make* you feel anything. If you think your child is 'making' you angry or your partner is 'making' you feel annoyed, remind yourself: **I choose my feelings.** It's an empowering mantra and worth writing down so you see it every day.

Your child's happiness doesn't depend on you, but until they have the emotional maturity to realise this and to choose their own feelings, your happiness will very much affect theirs.

Your emotions are your indicator, helping you to know whether your choice of thoughts and actions is taking you in the direction you want to go or not. In her book *Ask and It Is Given*, Esther Hicks encourages us to pay closer attention to our emotions and use them as a guide. She points out that when the fuel gauge on your car indicates that the tank is running empty, you don't criticise the indicator. You do something about adding more fuel to the tank. Similarly, a negative feeling is simply an indicator that your current choice of thoughts is not giving you your best energy. Notice your emotions, pay attention to the way you feel and appreciate your amazing indicator system.

Climb up the emotional ladder

Imagine a ladder with a range of emotions, the top rungs being things like joy/ love/appreciation/enthusiasm/optimism, and the middle section being boredom/

pessimism/frustration/impatience/irritation, then the lower rungs going from doubt/worry/blame/discouragement all the way down to anger/hatred/jealousy/fear/grief/depression.

As you move through your day, notice your emotions and where they fall on this ladder. Rather than attempting to snap yourself out of negative feelings and into a great mood immediately (which you probably can't), think about bringing yourself up one rung on the ladder at a time. You can do this by reaching for a better-feeling thought. Tell yourself, 'I want to feel good and I will try to feel good by choosing a thought that *does* feel good.'

Here's an example of how I've used this technique:

I was at the supermarket doing a huge food shop ahead of friends arriving to stay. When I reached the check-out, the queue was a mile long and moving at a snail's pace. It was clear I'd have no time to go home and unpack the bags before my school run. I imagined the ice cream melting, the milk going sour and the possibility of me being late to collect the kids. My chest tightened and my forehead began throbbing as I mentally cursed the supermarket management for not opening up more tills. I finally reminded myself: 'I choose my thoughts. No one is making me stressed right now. I'm choosing to be stressed.'

I'd be kidding myself if I thought at this point that I could just snap out of it, so I simply reached for a better-feeling thought. I looked at my shopping trolley, heaped with food, and thought, 'How fortunate am I to have such an abundance of food? There are people who would dream of being in my position right now. I feel incredibly grateful that I can open my wallet and pay for all of this.' I took a deep breath and let a feeling of genuine gratitude sweep over me. To pass the time further, I imagined how good the raspberries were going to taste. And how nice it would be to open that bottle of wine when my friends arrived.

I kept choosing better-feeling thoughts and, by the time I was unloading my items onto the belt, I was genuinely peaceful and calm. I didn't take any frustrations out on the cashier, but gave her a warm smile instead. On the way to school I replaced worry about being late with more pleasant thoughts. Imagine how differently I could have greeted my kids if I'd allowed my negative thinking to escalate into full-blown stress? And the potential knock-on effect that could have had on their own emotions?

In the past, before I understood the emotional ladder and my ability to choose my thoughts, I had countless days when I let my emotions spiral downwards instead of reaching for better-feeling thoughts. In times of deeper emotional difficulty it helps to write down where you are on the emotional ladder and why.

What are some ways you could lift yourself higher?

★ Play some feel-good music
★ Cuddle your child
★ Get some fresh air / surround yourself with nature
★ Eat something nourishing and healthy
★ Exercise
★ Meditate
★ Read an inspiring book
★ Write a list of 10 things you're feeling grateful for
★ Connect with an uplifting friend

Be careful about doing things that make you feel better temporarily – like having a drink or shopping – as the come down may be worse later. Do something that feels good now and will feel good all over again when you think about it later.

Mama Me Time

Mothers who make time for themselves are happier and more relaxed. And happier, more relaxed mothers = happier, more relaxed kids. If you're ever feeling a bit guilty about doing something for yourself, remember that you're doing it for your family too.

Creating some space in your life will allow you to be in better touch with yourself and how you're feeling. Yet it's hard when there's always so much else that needs doing. How can you relax and *not* think about the growing laundry pile or the fridge that needs refilling *again*?

Here's the truth: If you're running yourself ragged every day without coming up for much air, you're not going to be your best self. When you're not being your best self you don't like yourself much. When you don't like yourself you create 'bad weather' in your home. Your kids feel that and it affects their mood and how they behave.

One way to ensure your whole day doesn't fly past without any time to yourself is to have it first thing in the morning. If your child is no longer waking you up at ridiculous hours, it's well worth trying some morning Me Time.

I'd always convinced myself I was *not* a morning person, yet since I began setting my alarm for fifteen minutes before the kids wake up for school, I've never looked back. It was tempting at first to use that time to check emails and social media, or to get going on some jobs around the house, but I committed 100 per cent to using it as sacred Me Time. As my husband leaves for work very early, I stay under the covers and '*beditate*' to a guided meditation app, then write in my journal. Fifteen minutes no longer feels like enough time, so I now wake up half an hour earlier. Having this morning Me Time ritual is without a doubt the reason I now score my Personal Growth area high every month. It also makes me a much nicer mama on school mornings with my kids.

In the early years of motherhood, waking up early to meditate was the last thing on my mind. It was all about survival in those days! I used to try to find ways to grab just a couple of minutes of calm – anything to feel centred again and give myself the inner peace I needed to carry on till bedtime. I'd do a short yoga session with my boys climbing all over me and when that frustrated me (pretty much always!) I'd try and take a step back and realise that, messy as they were, those moments were beautiful and fleeting.

Now that my boys are older, it's a lot easier for me to get up before them. I love the peace-and-quiet feeling of having the world to myself. I cherish this time alone and on the rare occasion I don't get it, my day is guaranteed to turn out a lot more hectic.

I've dabbled in meditation for years, but it wasn't until Kelly introduced me to the Insight Timer meditation app that I finally established a consistent daily practice. It has impacted my life in so many ways. I'm more patient with my kids, kinder to myself, and recently I've made much better decisions about how I use my time. Before, when I had a lot of work on, I'd pop onto Facebook for a bit of light relief; now I choose meditation or a few yoga stretches over mindless scrolling every time.

Meditation has become a total pleasure for me and I'm a little bit addicted! Before, if I didn't get my daily Insight Timer fix, it'd be 'watch out for mama dinosaur!', but now I'm so familiar with the techniques that I can guide myself through a mini-meditation as I'm pulling my shoes on to run out the door or if I stop at traffic lights or have a couple of minutes to spare before pick-up.

My family know I meditate. My nine-year-old shares my love of Insight Timer and we often listen to a short one together at bedtime. All of the family definitely notice the benefits of a calm mummy. Now whenever I start getting grouchy they'll say, 'Go to your room and meditate!' It's a win-win!

–Louisa

Evening Me Time

If your day has flown past without doing anything for **you**, quality Me Time can happen in the evenings by setting a 'winding down' alarm and doing something to nurture yourself. I love to have a bath, light some candles, breathe and unwind before cosying up in bed with my journal, an inspiring book or a guided meditation. You don't have to do this every night, but if you've had a rough day, it'll feel like an indulgent treat and will set you up for a better day tomorrow.

Me Time Action Sheet

I've created a special Action Sheet to help you brainstorm a few things that will nourish you and feed your soul. You'll be more likely to choose a Me Time treat from your list rather than wasting it on social media, TV, tidying up or whatever your default mode is. On the following page I've listed some ideas from other mothers to get your juices flowing. Only you know what would feel like a Me Time treat for **you**.

Write your answers here, or print off a copy and hang it somewhere visible.

Get your Me Time Action Sheet from www.myprojectme.com/action-sheets.

Mama Me Time ideas

10 mins: Read a magazine (feet up!), sit in a sunny spot with a cup of tea, listen to a guided meditation app, breathe deeply with closed eyes, do some stretches, play music and dance, step outside and get some fresh air, stroke a pet, do some colouring in, read a chapter of a book, read some Project Me blogs, write a gratitude list, watch an inspiring TED Talk, eat a fruit salad – very slowly, appreciating the different colours and flavours.

30 mins: Read a few chapters of a book, take a walk, go for a run, do some more yoga stretches, do a longer meditation, listen to a podcast, journal, fill in a Project Me Action Sheet, do a mini home workout, call a friend for a catch-up, take a bath.

An hour: Paint your nails, take a walk in nature, go for a longer run or workout, ride a bike, meet a friend for coffee or a smoothie, read a longer section of your book, sit on a park bench and people-watch, do a full yoga session, scrapbook, bake, Project Me Hot Date With Myself.

Half a day/A whole day: Go to the hairdresser, meet a friend for an activity, eat out at a restaurant, get a manicure/pedicure, wander aimlessly, visit a gallery or exhibition, go window shopping, go clothes shopping, visit a yoga centre, attend a workshop, do an online course, get a massage or facial.

 **Project Me**

★ Me Time! ★

What would I do if I had 10 beautifully FREE minutes to myself?

And if I had 30 whole minutes...

What about an hour!?

Even more time... 2 hours, half a day, a WHOLE day!!!

From your fabulous brainstorm above, circle/highlight/star the ones that MOST appeal to you. Which would help you to feel happier and more like your best version of you? It's easy to spend your precious free time online (social media, trolling the web, emails), but is that nourishing you? YOU DECIDE.

I need regular ME time because:	Which obstacles might try to come between me and my deserved ME time?
How often will I create ME time in my day/week?	How can I overcome these obstacles?

Schedule in some ME Time for this week – and into the future.
Share this with your family so they can support you! YOU DESERVE THIS.

WWW.MYPROJECTME.COM

 oh yes!

Journaling

Do you keep a journal? Does the idea of opening a blank book and coming up with something to say sound daunting? Let go of the belief that you have to write anything interesting. It's for your eyes only and a great way to have a mental download about absolutely anything. Translating thoughts into writing helps you slow down, explore and process what's going on inside of you. Your journal can be your own best therapist.

Even though I've been keeping a journal on and off since I was ten, I didn't realise the true power of getting stuff out of my head and onto paper until two decades later. I began to deliberately use my journal as a tool to learn about myself and grow as a person. I could go back and read entries from previous years and recognise patterns of unhappiness and see which factors repeatedly caused me problems.

When you see it right there in black and white, in your own damn handwriting, it's hard to ignore. So I made changes where changes were needed and it wasn't always easy, but it worked. My journal writing is my biggest personal growth tool. I'll start a journal entry with, *Why am I feeling anxious/frustrated/overwhelmed/angry? What is this about?* – then see where it takes me. The answers always come once I use journaling to bring them out.

I have different journals on the go at once for various purposes. There's always my 'regular' journal, plus a travel journal that I take on trips to save any details I want to remember, including packing notes that'll help me for next time. I also keep a gratitude journal to remind me how much there *always* is to feel thankful for.

How to use a gratitude journal

Expressing gratitude in writing is a powerful tool and I use a special method I learned from Rhonda Byrne, author of *The Secret* and *The Magic*. Here's how it works:

Open a small notebook or journal and on the left side of the page write a few lines of gratitude for whatever you're feeling grateful for in your life right now, big or small – whatever comes to mind. Write, 'I'm so very thankful for _____ because _____.' Or 'Thank you so much for _____' and then a few words about why you're feeling grateful and what it means to you.

Then, on the right-hand page, write gratitude **in advance** for something you want. Write it in the present tense as if you already have it using the same format as before. Pause and let a smile spread across your face as you imagine how it will feel to read those words in the future and realise they've absolutely come true.

I've been doing this regularly now for several years and it's amazing to read through the right-hand entries in my old gratitude journals and see how this *really* works. Even seemingly far-fetched dreams have come true. I often do a double take at the date when I realise how far in advance I expressed heartfelt gratitude for something as if it was already in my life – like getting a publishing deal for this book you're reading right now!

If you decide to keep a gratitude journal, take note: psychology researchers have found that writing occasionally is more beneficial than writing daily for boosting happiness. There's no point turning it into a mechanically produced list without any conscious connection to what you're writing. Think of each thing you write about as a gift, relishing that feeling in your heart.

Glorious Goals!

As the Goal Diggers who've passed through my online courses know, I'm hugely into the power of goal setting. I've seen for myself how writing down what I want, then creating a small-step action plan works – and it's exciting to witness the successes of the women I've been privileged to work with. Having some clear goals to aim for gives you a sense of purpose and drive. You feel motivated and inspired to take action.

A goal without a plan of action is just a dream

Your goals don't have to be about climbing Mount Kilimanjaro or finishing a marathon – unless those truly are your aspirations! It's more about looking at your 8 Key Life Areas and thinking about what could make things flow better and bring you more day-to-day peace and happiness. The Project Me Life Wheel® is a great tool to help you get started on writing goals that'll improve whatever areas could use a boost.

Journal Prompt

My Dream Vision for the _____ area of my life:

★ How do I want this area of my life to look, feel and be? What would a score of nine or ten look like?
★ Why do I want this? How will it benefit me? My family?
★ What could happen if I do nothing?

Close your eyes and imagine it. How amazing will it feel when your Dream Vision becomes your reality? Write down any extra details that come to you. Once you vividly see what you're aiming for and deeply feel why you want it, it's time to identify one to three small-step actions you can take to get yourself off the starting blocks. You'll stay out of overwhelm if you break it down into micro actions and only focus on one small step at time.

Take Action!

Use an Ideas Into Action Sheet to capture any sparks of inspiration you found in the Personal Growth chapter. What are three small actions you can take straight away while it's all fresh in your mind?

Feeling stumped about how to make something work? Use a Challenge Solver Action Sheet to brainstorm any potential solutions.

All Project Me Action Sheets can be found at www.myprojectme.com/action-sheets.

BE THE BEST VERSION OF YOU

productivity

Productivity

As the **Mama CEO** (chief executive officer) of your family, investing time and energy into improving your productivity will pay off in more ways than you can imagine. Time management is really **life** management. In this chapter you'll learn to identify what's really important (and what's not), how to prioritise, get good systems in place and feel better-organised. This isn't about turning into a productivity robot who cares only about getting things done. Your expectations about what you can achieve in a day, week, month or even year need to be realistic depending on things like which stage of motherhood you're in, your health, and what kind of support you have.

Good productivity is a tool to help you free up more time to be present and connected to yourself and those you love. You'll be able to sense when your child or partner needs some attention. *Perhaps more than they need a sparkling clean house.* You'll also notice when your own motivation or energy levels are low. Take a breather rather than continuing to busy yourself with things that make you *feel* productive but aren't actually that important. It's OK to put your feet up sometimes without feeling guilty about it.

You are a human *being*, not a human *doing*

I spent years trying to deal with my constant state of overwhelm. I never knew where to start so I'd just start anywhere – and *then get nowhere.* I felt guilty for 'having it all' but not enjoying it because I was too frazzled to appreciate it. My poor kids bore the brunt of it. I didn't like the mean mama version of me that came out when I was tired and stressed. With a steely determination to turn things around for myself, I read every book I could get my hands on about time management, organisation and good habits. Creating better structure ultimately gave me more time and energy to devote to the things that are truly important to me. Now that I've got a good handle on this area of my life, I mentor mothers specifically with their productivity. I'm happy to share the tools and strategies that have turned things around for me in such a dramatic way.

Better Time Management

If you feel there are never enough hours in the day to do everything you want to be doing, let's explore this with a small (and cleverly effective) written exercise.

Grab a piece of paper or use the blanks below to write down **three things you don't have time for** – whatever comes to mind. Please don't read ahead or you'll be cheating yourself out of a valuable exercise.

1. I don't have time for _____.
2. I don't have time for _____.
3. I don't have time for _____.

Once you've done that, read on. (No peeking!)

(Pretend this space is some mellow *holding music* playing in the background as I wait for you to do this.)

Ready? OK.
Put your answers to each of the three questions above into the blanks below:

1. _____ is not important to me.
2. _____ is not important to me.
3. _____ is not important to me.

Now: **say your three new statements out loud**, three times for each sentence.

(I'll wait.)

Did that stir up any emotions?

Did any of them feel like uncomfortable or false statements? Could it be that maybe the *opposite* is true?

Often the first three things you think of are in fact things that *are* very important to you. They might be what's eating away at you inside, making you feel guilty, frustrated or unfulfilled.

If the statement felt true and it really *isn't* important to you, it's interesting to consider why you thought of it.

The point of this exercise is to help you recognise what matters to you and what you value.

When you ignore your values or put things that matter on the back burner for too long, you don't feel good. You might feel a tightness in your chest, a pit in your stomach or a swirling in your head when you think about it.

I'm all for dropping unnecessary guilt, but sometimes it's a signal to remind us to live by our values.

Forget about time management. This is **priority** management. Get clear about *why* you want to make time for these things. Focus on the outcome and how good you'll feel.

IT'S NOT ABOUT HAVING TIME, IT'S ABOUT MAKING TIME.

The disappearing time act

Back when my youngest child began nursery school, I was thrilled to have **three bonus hours a day** to get stuff done. I fantasised about how amazing my life would be with an additional **twelve hours a week**! But it wasn't long before I felt just as busy as ever.

Two years later when he started 'big school', I conjured up more images of what my life would look like with all of the 'extra' time I'd have. I'd get the house organised, create filing systems, make photo albums, finish the baby books, learn Spanish, train to be a yoga teacher . . . But that time evaporated too.

If you're dreaming about all of the 'extra hours' you'll have once your child starts school or returns to school after a break, here's the truth:

Your time expands or contracts to fill whatever you put into it. If you've got half an hour to do something, you'll do it in half an hour. If you have more time than that, you'll take longer to do it. Sometimes a *lot* longer.

We all have the same twenty-four hours in a day. Conscientiously choose what you fill your day with.

> I have a really hard time multi-tasking. If I start housework, I never get finished 'enough' to do anything else. I also have too many things I want to do for myself: scrapbook, work out, read, meal plan, parenting seminars, de-clutter and organise. Whenever I do have time for myself, I usually feel too overwhelmed to even pick one thing to do so I just sleep or surf the internet. The only way I can imagine changing this is to go live by myself!! Kidding . . . sort of.
> —Amanda

I CAN DO ANYTHING

BUT NOT *EVERY*THING.

Where is your time actually going?

This next exercise is designed to help you see more objectively how you spend your time. I'll never forget the flash of 'Eureka!' I had when this was introduced to me during my parenting skills course with The Parent Practice. It ultimately changed my life.

Parenting coach Elaine Halligan drew a grid on her flipchart and asked the mothers in the room to tell her what had filled our previous couple of days. She put our answers into one of four quadrants.

The **Important/Urgent** quadrant is for anything with an imminent deadline, a crisis, an emergency – or important things left until the last minute. Our examples included things like: taking a sick child to the doctor, finding an emergency call-out plumber, buying food for dinner that night, finding a costume for the school play that week, buying a birthday present on the way to the party, paying an overdue bill, returning something to a shop on the very last day to get a refund. *Notice how many of those things became urgent because they weren't done earlier.*

Important/Not Urgent is where good time managers spend the most time, yet most of us don't. When we procrastinate and leave things until the last minute, they slide from this quadrant over to 'urgent' and that's what makes us feel like headless chickens.

Doing important things before they become urgent is the key. This is also the area for planning ahead and proactive problem solving. It's important, yet, because it's not urgent, it might not happen – unless you put your mind to it. Reading this book and completing the Action Sheets is a great example of operating from this quadrant. Nurturing your important relationships also goes into this area, including your relationship with yourself. *Self-care might never feel urgent, but it's incredibly important.*

Think of the **Not Important/Not Urgent** quadrant as being filled with your favourite time-sucks and also anything that keeps you *feeling* busy, but isn't actually as important as it seems at the time. For example: checking your inbox or social media a billion times a day, doing endless research before making a decision, mooching around the shops longer than you need to. This is not to say that you can never have any down time just doing nothing. Or that you can't use social media, read a magazine or watch TV. It's just about being more self-aware about when you *choose* to do these things so that you aren't operating on autopilot and then complaining that you *never have enough time.*

The **Not Important/Urgent** quadrant is for dealing with other people's urgencies, which are not at the top of your *own* personal to-do list. Examples include dashing to school to deliver a forgotten homework assignment, or taking on something for someone else because you find it hard to say no. It's also for interruptions, like your kids arguing when you're trying to get something done in another room. These kinds of things trick you because they can feel important at the time. Once you begin to recognise them as belonging in this lower left-hand quadrant, you'll begin to reduce some of them. Parenting skills classes helped me to stop rescuing my kids when they forgot things (which meant they stopped forgetting things), and ended the sibling squabbles that sucked up much of my time and energy.

My biggest light bulb-over-the-head moment (which ultimately changed my career path) was the realisation that 80 per cent of my time as a freelance graphic designer was spent in the Not Important/Urgent quadrant. I was dealing with other people's urgent deadlines all of the time. It didn't matter how much I improved my own time management if my clients were always leaving things until the last minute, then relying on me to pull out all the stops to meet *their* deadlines. I was spending money on childcare on the days I worked, only to be left waiting for approval on my artwork – twiddling my thumbs for non-billable hours. Then on my day off, just as I was heading to the park with my little one, they'd ring with some changes that needed to be done **urgently**!

This revelation prompted me to take a hiatus for a few months. I wanted to be able to implement what I'd learned in my parenting skills classes and to start doing the things I never had time to do: organise photos, finish my second child's baby book, get my recipes in order, start meal planning, clear the clutter and sell stuff. I wanted to get my house and my life in order, which was something important to **me**.

This was the start of my Project Me and I never went back to freelance graphic design. Thankfully other people's urgent deadlines rarely take up my time any more.

Take Action!

Now it's your turn. Use this blank grid to fill in the things you've done over the last few days, or quickly draw up your own. Pat yourself on the back for all that you do which is Important/Not Urgent. How often are you doing Important/Urgent things? Could you reduce those by giving yourself earlier deadlines? Or by planning and problem solving? What about other people's urgencies and interruptions? Do you spot any time-sucks or when you're keeping busy for busy's sake? How can you reduce these things?

urgent   not urgent

important

not important

Soon you'll begin to recognise the seemingly important stuff that may not be in alignment with your values. Sometimes you have to step away from it to see it with fresh eyes.

Awareness is the first step to change.

Master Your To-Do List

If you're still scribbling your to-dos on the backs of envelopes, sticky notes or keeping it all in your head it's no wonder you're feeling frazzled and unfocused. Anyone who thinks, 'I don't need to write it down because I'll remember it' is setting themself up for trouble. **Out of your head and onto paper!**

The first step is to have a gigantic brain-dump of all of those to-dos that have been clogging up your busy brain.

What's keeping you up at night? Making you feel guilty because you never get around to doing it? Anything you need to get done for you, your family, work . . . This week, next week, long-term . . . What about those goals and dreams you never get off the ground?

Gather up all sticky notes, scraps of paper and half-written to-do lists, and organise them into one central place. It helps to create a general task list, then other sections for home projects, things for the kids, things just for you.

Two top tips I always give in my Master Your To-Do List workshop

1. Begin each task with a verb and a clear description.
2. Anything that can't be completed as a single task needs to be thought of as a project. Break it down into small, baby steps. What would be the first thing you'd do to get started? And after that?

Inside of a busy mama's head.

Here are those same thoughts written down very specifically with verbs. All projects are broken down into first steps:

☐ Book dentist appointments for kids and me
☐ Meal plan
☐ Download the Insight Timer meditation app onto my phone

Project: Birthday Party
☐ 1. Make guest list
☐ 2. Write and send invites

Project: My passport renewal
☐ Download application form
☐ Complete form
☐ Gather supporting documents
☐ Get passport photo taken

Project: Make photo albums
☐ List the photo albums I want to create
☐ Make folders for the photos for first album

Now your brain can quickly scan your to-do list and know exactly what needs doing without wasting any processing time. It'll also save you from procrastinating over things that seem too overwhelming. You may be dragging your feet on getting your passport application started because you can't stop thinking about getting your photo taken. By starting with a different aspect of the process you'll get off the starting blocks – and won't be pulling your hair out by leaving it until you're about to travel.

Many women I work with feel buried by the thought of their 'never-ending' to-do list. I encourage them to embrace it. Yes, your to-do list *is* never-ending! You're a vibrant woman living a full life with lots of things you need and want to do. Would you rather be twiddling your thumbs in boredom? Embrace who you are and that wonderfully endless list of things to do.

Take Action!

Have a brain-dump by writing down everything that needs doing, all in one centralised place.

Begin each task with a verb and get specific.

Break all projects down into smaller step-by-step tasks.

Carrie booked a Skype session with me to address her Productivity and time management struggles. She said:

I have a constant feeling of overwhelm with never-ending to-do lists. I just feel like I'm spinning in circles, addressing the constant 'fires' and not really accomplishing anything. I feel like I get further behind every day instead of making headway.

Together we looked at her many to-do lists and got them all centralised into one place, categorising and ordering them by priority, and breaking bigger projects down into step-by-step tasks. Next we looked carefully at how she was spending her time and we quickly identified that she was working on her home business far too late into the evenings. As I know first-hand what sleep deprivation does to our state of mind, I gave Carrie a 'get to bed earlier' challenge.

I checked back with her two weeks later and she was a different person:

It feels so good to have a central place to keep track of my to-dos. I love being able to mark things as done! My sense of complete overwhelm has diminished, it all feels more manageable – and I know it will only get better! I'm getting to bed earlier and am far more productive with my work.

I TAKE
SMALL STEPS
EVERY DAY.

THERE!
ME
GET
WILL
STEPS
STEADY
SMALL

Overcome Overwhelm

Now that you've got your tasks and projects in one place, do you feel better – or is your head in a spin over where to begin? Does it feel like **everything** has to be done **now**? How do you start to prioritise?

I've got a magic wand to make it better – my **Magic Matrix** Action Sheet.

This is based on the grid you used earlier to think about where you're spending most of your time. Now you'll use it to understand what's **really** important and urgent on your to-do list, what can wait and what could be delegated.

'But it all feels important and urgent!' I hear you cry.

It won't feel that way once you've done this:

Step 1: Print a Magic Matrix Action Sheet (or draw the grid on the nearest piece of paper). You can also use coloured pens on your actual list.

Step 2: Put your tasks into the relevant quadrants.

Q1. Important and Urgent

This is the JUST DO IT box. If a task needs doing today or at the latest tomorrow, and only you can do it, put it here. Having too much stuff in this box is stressful and puts you in crazy-mama mode. You ideally want this box to be empty most days – so clear this section first.

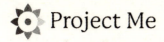 Project Me

 ★ Magic Matrix ★

For overcoming overwhelm and
knowing what to do first.

Put your tasks into the relevant quadrants. (Everything on your list AND in your head).

Q1. Important and Urgent	**Q2.** Important but Not Urgent (yet)
Q3. Not Important and Not Urgent (push it back!)	**Q4.** Delegate

WWW.MYPROJECTME.COM

Q2. Important but Not Urgent (yet)

If it's not screamingly urgent *yet*, but **will** be if you procrastinate – put it here. This quadrant is also the place for planning, organisation and self-care. It's where you want to spend most of your time each day.

Examples: paying bills, booking travel, making appointments, meal planning, figuring challenges out on paper, working on your Project Me.

Q3. Not Important and Not Urgent (but you still really want to do it!)

Put stuff here that you don't want to forget and it'll stay on your radar. Later, when you're out of overwhelm, start to break bigger projects down into smaller steps so you can block off small chunks of time to make some headway on them.

Examples: clearing the clutter, home decorating projects, a wardrobe rehaul, organising photos, crafting/hobbies.

Once you've identified it as not urgent or important right now, **stop thinking about it**. This is the ticket to getting out of overwhelm. It's here on your list and doesn't need to be taking up room in your brain.

Q4. Delegate

When your head's in a spin and you've got waaaay too much on your plate, it's time to delegate. Don't be a martyr. Ask for help. It's all about *how* you ask. Can another mother from school collect your kids? Could a friend run an errand for you at the same time as she's running her own? Can your hubby/kids pitch in? If you admit you're snowed under and you ask nicely, people are generally happy to help out.

> *As a young mother dealing with depression, the Project Me tools have allowed me to get organized and build routines that I've needed for so long. These have been crucial to helping me get back on my feet. I'm so thankful for all of your help!*
> **—Aletha**

Use the Magic Matrix technique to clear your cluttered brain and give you some perspective on what you need to focus on *now* – and what can wait.

Going forward, use your Q2 time wisely. Operating within this quadrant is the key to feeling less like a headless chicken and more like a productivity ninja. When life throws you a Q1 style curveball (which it will) you'll have the time and headspace to deal with it more easily.

I worked with Fiona to help her with the Productivity area of her life. She was prone to procrastination and only did things once they became Important and Urgent. By showing her a way of managing her to-do list using the Magic Matrix concept, things improved quickly. She wrote to say:

I'm so much more organised and clear about my priorities thanks to your encouragement and motivation. I've taken my head out of the sand and now have the confidence to take on other things, like the parenting skills class I never had time for before. This is a definite life changer.

Design Your Day

With your master to-do list at the ready, it's time to design your days with intention. No more diving in blindly without a clear game plan, doing whatever's in front of your face, flying wildly off-piste and then beating yourself up for everything that's fallen through the cracks – again.

The absolute number one way I stay focused and get the right stuff done is by using a **Design My Day** Action Sheet every day.

I'll walk you through each section of Design My Day here:

1. Give gratitude.

Jot a short note about whatever you're feeling particularly grateful for today. A daily practice of feeling gratitude for what you already have brings more good stuff into your life. Really!

2. Choose your feelings.

We spend too much time thinking of what we have to *do* and not enough on how we want to *feel* when we're doing it.

Write three words that best describe how you'd like to feel today. If your day ahead is jam packed, you might choose to feel: *Calm. Peaceful. Mindful.* With those desired feelings guiding your day, you'll get it done in a better frame of mind.

For a family day at home, you may choose to feel: *Connected. Present. Playful.*

Is someone in your life driving you nuts? You might want to feel: *Patient. Loving. Kind.*

I often choose the word FLOW as I know that when I approach my to-dos with a sense of flow, it all feels more effortless.

✿ Project Me

★ Design My Day ★

Today I'm grateful for

Today I will feel

SCHEDULED EVENTS

Time	Event (what's already planned?)	Prepare for success (what to remember, what to take with me etc.)

TODAY'S 3 MITS (Most Important Tasks)

1. .... ☐
2. .... ☐
3. .... ☐

AFTER MY 3 MITS (if there's time...)

1. .... ☐
2. .... ☐
3. .... ☐
4. .... ☐
5. .... ☐

PHONE CALLS / EMAILS

1. .... ☐
2. .... ☐
3. .... ☐
4. .... ☐
5. .... ☐

focus!

WWW.MYPROJECTME.COM

3. Schedule in events and prepare for success.

Refer to your calendar and jot down where you have to be today and when. What can you do to make it all go smoothly? Do you need to take snacks and a swimming bag for the lesson, forms to the appointment, retainer to the orthodontist, eco bags to the supermarket? Park it all by the front door so you're not flying around last-minute.

Leave some gaps so you can slot in some other things . . . Could you prep dinner earlier? Run an errand on the way to school? Think about ways to prepare for a smooth and successful day.

4. Identify your three most important tasks.

Your three MITs are the tasks you most want or need to get done today. Check your to-do list and if there's anything Important and Urgent (i.e. it must be done today or tomorrow at the latest), make it one of your three MITs. If not, choose something that has a deadline coming up and get it out of the way so it doesn't become urgent. It's also a good idea to choose a small-step action towards one of your goals to ensure you make steady progress.

Focus on doing your chosen three MITs **first** before you get sucked into anything else. You have the most focus and energy at the start of your day and leaving it until later means a much greater chance something else will get in the way.

5. Add a few more things from your to-do list.

Once you've done your three MITs, what else would be great to get done today? You might not get to all (or any) of these, but it's good to have something to aim for. Remember – even if something's not urgent yet, it's good to get it done now before it *becomes* urgent. Often I need to carry tasks in this section over to the next day, but as long as I get my three MITs done, I feel a great sense of accomplishment.

6. Phone calls and emails.

Instead of making phone calls throughout the day, note the calls you need to make and do them all at once. Stay out of your inbox as much as possible and set a time limit once you do go in. Write down anyone you need to email and send those mails before you get caught up in fresh ones. I know, easier said than done . . .

There's a nice white space at the bottom for all of those extra thoughts and notes that pop up throughout the day. You can refer to those when designing your next day. **Important note:** A mother's life is **unpredictable**. Just when you're getting started on your first MIT, you get a call from the school nurse and have to drop everything. Try to see unforeseen setbacks as opportunities to model flexibility to your children. The earlier they learn to adapt to altered plans the better. Do your best and stop beating yourself up for not getting it ALL done. Never be a slave to your to-do list. Feeling love and finding joy in each day is what's truly important.

Extra Time Management Tips

Create an ongoing errands list and batch them together so you're not always heading off to the shops.

Practise saying no to people and things that aren't a priority for you. When you say yes to others, make sure you're not saying no to yourself.

Pay attention to your time-leaks. When you spend time doing mindless stuff that isn't even fulfilling, you're taking away from the meaningful things that would make a positive difference in your life.

Take Action!

Even if you normally use another planner, I encourage you to print out two weeks' worth of the Design My Day Action Sheets and see what kind of difference it makes to your life. Remember that all Action Sheets are located at www.myprojectme.com/action-sheets.

Here's a small sample of the positive feedback I've had from mothers who are now designing their days:

> The DMD sheets are a real godsend! They help organise my thoughts for the day ahead, cutting through the clutter and brain fog! I always do one the night before as it suits my night owl tendencies – then hit the ground running the next day. My son calls them my 'mummy planner'.
> **–Louise**
>
> Design My Day is a life-saver!!! It helps me feel more organised and productive. I fill some tasks out at the end of my workday and then add more in the morning so I know what to focus on and don't feel like I will forget anything.
> **–Daniela**
>
> I love the Design my Day sheet. It helps me focus on what is really important. And be kinder to myself too . . . no worries if I do only two tasks that day . . . sometimes less is better. And I can dedicate more time to myself.
> **–Sophie**
>
> Design My Day is life-changing. It really helps me to focus on what I need to do, instead of drifting through the day with a vague list of things in my head. Writing things down makes a HUGE difference!
> **–Abbie**

Procrastination Busting

Are you a pro procrastinator? Got stuff on your to-do list that's been hanging around forever? Half-started projects lingering around indefinitely? Are you the Queen of Putting It Off?

A Project Me survey revealed that procrastination is a top struggle we all face. It either induces guilt or puts you under a crazy amount of pressure by leaving things until the last minute.

Having stuff on your to-do list for days/weeks/months weighs you down, nags at you and makes you feel guilty.

So how do you stop *thinking* about it and just do it?

1. Ask yourself – is it really important?

You need to know *why* you want to do something to have a deep enough motivation to actually do it. If you decide that it's really NOT important, wipe it off your list – and out of your mind.

2. Power through it.

If it *is* important and there's a deadline attached to it – just do it *before* it becomes urgent. When you put things off until the last minute all of the time, you're in firefighting mode. Plug away at the important but not urgent (yet) stuff to create a calmer life for yourself. Set your three MITs (most important tasks) each day and do those things first!

3. Break it down.

Maybe you're not cracking on with something because it feels overwhelming or like it'll take too much time? Chunk it into smaller steps and *just take the first one*. This works especially well with projects. Create a step-by-step game plan with deadlines for each step – and schedule them into your calendar. *This really does work!*

4. Eliminate distractions.

'I'll get started as soon as I've checked Facebook and emails . . .' Identify your typical distractions and beat them at their own game. Turn off all notifications, resist urges, be strong. (Yes, small children are distractions, but I'm not suggesting you should eliminate them . . .)

5. Find a motivation buddy.

Tired of dragging your feet on certain tasks or projects that you want to do, but never make time for? Enlist a friend who'll accept no excuses. The power of accountability is not to be underestimated. Talk it through with them, tell them what steps you'll take and when you'll do them by. Meeting up once a month with a Power Pal is an amazing way to get added accountability and a motivational push in the right direction.

Stop labelling yourself as a procrastinator. Consider yourself a doer!

Be sure to recognise the difference between procrastination and honestly needing a rest. You'll be more productive if you balance doing with being. *Push less and flow more.*

I am
THE CEO
of my family

All Systems GO!

Becoming the expert and CEO of your family means sitting down and putting systems into place that will make the things you need to do regularly go more seamlessly. You may want to devise a system for house cleaning or paying bills, or create a family calendar for keeping track of everyone's activities. There's no definitive way. Simply sit down and figure it out on paper, then give it a whirl – tweaking as needed until it works.

Weekly meal planning is a system that makes my life much easier. Whenever I'm tempted to go food shopping without a plan I have to remind myself that it's a waste of time. I buy random stuff and within two days I run out of crucial ingredients to make a proper meal – and have to do another food shop. When I meal plan on Sunday for the week ahead I'm always so glad I did.

When planning your meals, consider what the week ahead looks like for you and your family. Do you have a travelling partner or guests coming over? Are you out for dinner any evenings? Do the kids have extracurricular activities or play dates? Are there days you'll be running around with no time to prep? Planning meals around your schedule and lifestyle is the key to success.

I'm sharing my **Weekly Meal Planner** with you on the Action Sheets download page: www.myprojectme.com/actionsheets. Grab as many as you need to set up your own system for weekly meal planning. You'll also find a blank grid for creating your own charts, systems or lists.

Project Me

★ Weekly Meal Planner ★

MONDAY

TUESDAY

WEDNESDAY

THURSDAY

FRIDAY

SATURDAY

SUNDAY

NOTES:

yum!

Clear the Clutter

Home organisation is another aspect of Productivity that can wear you down if you aren't on top of it. A cluttered house creates a cluttered mind. You'll feel incredibly lighter once you've had a good clear-out. You also save yourself time when everything is in its right place instead of always having to look for things.

When I worked with a client to help her with the Productivity area of her life, she said that her biggest struggle was living in a cluttered house and feeling utterly overwhelmed and paralysed with where to begin. After digging deep she got to the bottom of her problem. Her own mother was a neat freak who cared more about a tidy house than giving her kids love and affection. She vowed not to be like her mother, but the clutter in her home drags her down so much emotionally that she's not actually being the mother she wants to be. Her light bulb-over-the-head insight was realising that it doesn't have to be one or the other. She can get rid of clutter and still heap loads of love on her kids. She's now experiencing the emotional freedom that comes from clearing the clutter in her home.

My own mother gave up material possessions to live a life on the road doing volunteer work in exchange for room and board. Her motto: **'You don't own stuff, stuff owns you.'** She lives a life of freedom that a lot of people dream of. Not everyone needs to go to the minimalist extreme, but most of us could do with owning a lot less.

Avoid overwhelm and procrastination by decluttering your home in small steps. I found the book *The Life-Changing Magic of Tidying* by Marie Kondo very useful when we downsized homes. I recommend her method of gathering all like items together in one place so you can see how many similar things you have. Then you hold each piece in your hand and ask yourself, 'Does this spark joy?' Anything that doesn't spark joy goes! Kondo's book helps with the emotions around de-cluttering, such as what to do with things other people have gifted you or how to get rid of something that has sentimental value but is no longer sparking joy. She has a method of finding a set place for everything you own and always returning things to their place. This is the key to not having to tidy constantly – which sounds good to me. If only I could get the rest of my family on board.

Take Action!

Choose a small area of your house to tackle – even one drawer. By clearing the clutter in small, doable chunks of time, you'll build momentum and feel ready to take on the bigger stuff next.

Assemble Your Support Squad

Are you tired of feeling like the family slave? Do you feel as though, if you don't do it yourself, it'll *never* get done? Wish your kids would pitch in and help, but feel like they're too young or it's not worth the battle trying to get them to do it?

Many mothers resist asking for help, thinking they have to do everything themselves. They become martyrs, believing that the more they sacrifice for their kids the better mothers they are. They never sit down, as there's always something else that needs doing. Over time, the Martyr Mother becomes resentful. She begrudges her family for leaving her to do everything, yet she's been doing it for so long that no one thinks to offer their help.

If you recognise this in yourself, imagine the build-up over time – with teenagers who don't clean up after themselves and you doing everything for everyone else and nothing for you. It's best to nip this in the bud now. Let go of the feeling that it's your job to do everything and start to ASK for help. Support won't come unless you ask for it.

This means letting go of perfection and thinking that no one else will do it as well as you do. Maybe they won't. So what?

A strong Mama CEO needs to assemble her support squad and learn the art of delegation.

Support from your kids

In a survey I conducted amongst my Project Me newsletter subscribers, I asked: 'Does your child/children have weekly or daily chores to help out around the house?'

49 per cent said no. The two most common reasons were: 1. I don't ask for it. 2. My kids are too young.

It was interesting to note how many mothers with kids aged between five and eight thought their kids were too young.

Little kids *want* to help and they can do it from a much younger age than you think. Sure, in the beginning it's going to feel *a lot* easier/faster/more efficient to do it all yourself, but teaching and training them young gets them into a naturally helpful mindset and you'll *save* yourself a lot of time, nagging and resentment later on.

If your child is older and has never had specific jobs to do around the house, help to send them off into the world with a set of basic skills and good habits they'll use for the rest of their life. Their future roommates and spouses will appreciate it too!

By doing too much for your child, you're denying them an opportunity to practise self-reliance.

Remember this the next time you're tempted to do something simple that they could be doing for themselves.

Support from your partner

Feeling peeved that your partner's not pulling their weight on the domestic front? Constantly nagging and feeling resentful that they just don't see what needs doing and pitch in *without being asked*?

It's frustrating to live under the same roof as a fully capable adult, yet feel like you've got another person to pick up after. Resentment builds up until it drives a serious wedge between you. Studies show that couples fight more over who does the most cooking and cleaning than anything else – except money.

The very first step is to identify the issues and do a little review of how it got to this point in the first place.

Did your partner help out more in the past? When and why did things shift? Are you feeling hard done by and resentful over the whole big picture, or are there specific tasks or situations that push your buttons? For example, do weekends trigger you – when you're both at home and it feels like just another weekday to you because you're doing everything? Or do you just wish they'd be proactive and tidy up after meals and run the dishwasher? Or cook at least one meal a week, do a food shop, or entertain the kids?

Have you been unintentionally training them *not* to help out? If you've repeatedly criticised their way of doing things or taken over and done it yourself, your partner may have stopped bothering to try. Do you feel guilty asking for help when you '*should*' be the one doing it? Pause and accept your own possible role in it.

It's also a good idea to think about the things they *do* do. Couples are known to perceive their own contributions as being more valuable than their partners', with both sides believing they're doing the majority of the work.

Use a Challenge Solver Action Sheet to write down what the specific issues are. What do you specifically want help with? *You don't ask, you don't get.*

Getting outside support

If you can afford to pay someone, consider what you could outsource. Look at everything that needs doing and choose your least favourite tasks to delegate. For me it's always been laundry, changing the bedding and ironing my husband's work shirts. Paying for help doesn't feel weird to me. As a teenager I earned money by helping a harassed mother in my neighbourhood, by cleaning her house and babysitting. I used the money to help pay my university fees. When I became a mother myself it came naturally for me to hire help from girls needing to earn money. Three of the girls who've worked for me are now grown-up mothers themselves.

Journal Prompt

★ What are my mental blocks or excuses around asking for or accepting help?

★ What kinds of things would I like more help with?

★ Who could I ask? Where can I look for help?

When you gain clarity over what you want and you allow yourself to imagine it, the solution often appears. Once you've got some support, be patient and drop perfection. It can take time to teach and train someone else to help you, but it'll free you up to do those things you said you never have time for.

Take Action!

Use an Ideas Into Action Sheet to identify one small step you can take this week towards prioritising something that's important to you. What are the next two steps after that?

If you know what to do, schedule it in. If it needs working out, use a Challenge Solver Action Sheet. Don't try to figure this out in your head. The act of writing down what you want will slow down your busy brain and the answers will come to you. Do it and see what happens!

All Project Me Action Sheets can be found at www.myprojectme.com/action-sheets.

family

Family

As a mother it may feel like the Family area is the centre of your life with everything else revolving around it. And in many ways it is. The early days of motherhood are all-consuming and can take up every ounce of your energy. No decision is made without considering how it fits in around your precious little one. As you move out of that stage, it's good to shift your perspective so that YOU are at the centre and your child or children are an extension of that. Don't lose your SELF completely to motherhood. Family is but one petal on your Life Wheel.

If you're past the baby and toddler stage and it continues to feel as if this is the most energy-consuming area of your life, it's time to do an assessment of why. Perhaps you could shift your attention to some other areas of your life to help you find your balance. It could be that when you focus more on your Personal Growth or your Health, you find ways to manage it all more easily.

Maybe a specific part of your family life needs figuring out? Creating a firm foundation is important and often needs an **investment of focused attention**. I found this out for myself the hard way.

My Family Life was a Hot Mess

My two-year-old ruled the roost and didn't listen to a word I said. He and my five-year-old squabbled incessantly. I felt like I was losing my mind.

My husband and I disagreed over discipline and ended up having huge arguments in front of the kids. I remember him slamming the front door behind him as he left on a business trip, saying he couldn't wait to get out of there. I sank to the floor and bawled my eyes out.

This wasn't the happy family life I'd envisioned. No one told me it would be so hard. In fact, everyone else was making it look easy. Maybe I wasn't cut out to be a mother? I didn't seem to be made from the right stuff.

I'm ashamed to admit that I took my frustrations out on my kids. I overreacted, shouted, punished, and I was heavy-handed with them more than once. My kids deserved better, but I had no idea how to change things. I read some books on discipline and parenting, but didn't manage to implement anything that made a difference.

One day I spotted an ad for a parenting skills workshop run by The Parent Practice near my home. I went along for a free taster class, unsure if I'd actually commit to the money or time of the full ten-week course. I found myself surrounded by mothers who were also finding parenting tough. I realised I was not alone and that there were many ways to make things better.

I used to think that everything was my kids' fault, but soon I figured out that changing my own behaviour improved their behaviour too. Within a few weeks of concentrating on my parenting skills, my boys were happily playing with each other, following through on instructions, and our home took on a whole different, happier vibe. I learned how to problem solve and I discovered the importance of setting some time aside each week to plan, organise and prepare for success.

If you'd told me back then that I'd one day go on to work with The Parent Practice, helping other stressed-out mothers get a handle on their family life, I'd have honestly laughed in your face. *Me* helping anyone else with *their* kids? But within a few short months that's exactly what I was doing.

My boys are now teenagers and incredibly respectful and lovely to be around. Once I got past all of the behavioural difficulties, I was able to forge a deep, meaningful relationship with them and encourage their sense of values, ethics and communication. *If I were still screaming at them every day, I don't know if they'd be able to shine the way they do.*

The investments of money, time and energy I made have paid off for all of us. They freed me up to devote attention to other areas of my life. I did a life-coaching course, started my own business, and my husband and I stopped fighting over the kids and went back to being best friends.

You can continue to wing it, or you can give yourself the chance to enjoy your children – bringing them up with your family values, instead of always just putting out fires. Don't give yourself (or your kids) a hard time. Get all the support you can. Fortunately, parenting skills can be learned and mindsets can be changed.

Parenting is personal

There's no one-size-fits-all plan when it comes to how to raise your children. Educate yourself with different points of view and hone in on what feels right for you. The worst thing you can do is nothing.

Become the expert of your family. Once you discover what works for your family, you will troubleshoot and defer problems before they turn into major issues. You'll free yourself up to enjoy motherhood more.

It's easy to look around at other mothers and think that everyone else is finding it much smoother. You might wonder why it's only you who seems to have these problems or it's only your child who behaves this way.

Please know you're not alone in your journey. Many women suffer through their problems privately and put on a brave face in public. They don't want to admit that they feel like a bad mother or that they don't have a handle on their kids. They feel guilty and stressed. I know, because I definitely used to feel this way.

I'm going to share a few stories of the specific struggles I faced and how I overcame them. If something doesn't feel right for you or your family, start thinking about what would work. You can figure anything out if you put your mind to it.

How to Stop Shouting at Your Kids

Do you ever hear yourself shouting at your kids to **'Stop shouting'**? The irony isn't lost on me. I am a recovering shout-aholic. When my boys were younger I'd have a sore throat from turbulent episodes of unleashed fury.

I knew I should be counting to ten and taking deep breaths, yet my explosions were so quick to rise that I never seemed to have time for that.

Things needed to change. I had to do something.

Here's what finally worked:

1. **Recognise stress triggers.**

   It helped enormously to be aware of the typical situations and times of day I was prone to losing my rag. I identified my biggest triggers as getting out the door in the mornings and being ready and on time for swimming lessons. I also noticed that late in the day I was more likely to be a mama on a very short fuse. Knowing all of this helped me prepare for success by making sure clothes, book bags and swimming kits were ready the night before. I stopped having the radio on in the kitchen at breakfast, eliminating my frustration over my kids talking over what was being said. I would have also used a meditation app to reset myself before the evening routines – if apps had existed back then!

2. **Learn to apologise.**

   This was a tough one for me. In my mind *they'd* caused me to get angry, so it wasn't *my* fault I ended up shouting. I made a firm pact with myself that if I ever shouted I *had* to apologise, no matter what. I don't like apologising, so I became much more mindful about not shouting.

3. Be in the present moment.

I'm more prone to outbursts when a deep train of thought is interrupted. To the kids it might have looked like I was just stirring the pasta sauce, but in my mind I was trying to figure something out. Being asked when dinner would be ready triggered me to shout that it would be ready a lot faster if they'd stop interrupting me (*ouch*)! Keeping my mind in the 'now' and being fully present for my children truly helps. I do my deep thinking when they're not around and use a Challenge Solver Action Sheet or my journal to figure things out on paper.

4. Create a mantra.

Mine is: 'My child is not *being* a problem, my child is *having* a problem.' I've had that mantra on a sticky note on my wall ever since my kids were small, and it helps me to take a deep breath and reframe the situation. It comes from Bonnie Harris, author of *When Kids Push Your Buttons and What You Can Do About It.* Bonnie reminds us that **all behaviour is caused**. Your child is not deliberately trying to wind you up. *Honestly!* Even if it feels that way, remember that your child is not *being* a problem, they are *having* a problem. This shifts you out of explosive reactionary mode and into a softer place. After all, if your child is having a problem, you're going to feel more compassionate and it puts you into problem solving instead of punishment mode.

Emotional States

thinking

thinking

feeling

feeling

NORMAL STATE

UPSET STATE

Think of your mind as being like the eggs in this diagram. In a normal state, you have a nice balance between thinking and feeling. When you get upset, the egg (your mind) gets too filled up with emotion and there's very little room left for thinking. All rationality goes out the window!

This is why, even when we know what we should be doing or saying when our child misbehaves, we can't access it when we're too filled up with emotion.

See? There's a scientific explanation and there's actually nothing wrong with you! The same goes for our children. It's pointless to try to reason with an overly emotional child. Wait until their egg has evened out before attempting to talk sense with them or you're just wasting your time and energy.

How to Get Your Child to Listen to You – The First Time

Do you feel a broken record – repeating the same instruction to your child over and over?

I used to go nuts over my boys' inability to hear me. I got louder and louder until I'd morphed into a crazed chronic shout-aholic. Things got really out of control. At The Parent Practice I learned the secret for getting my kids to listen to me the *first* time I say it.

Kids have selective hearing. They tune out the sound of your voice unless it's something they *want* to hear. You may have noticed husbands suffer this same affliction . . .

So what do we do? We repeat.

'Sam, I told you to put on your shoes. We're leaving **now**.'

And we repeat again, louder and more annoyed. And again, this time with exasperation, then anger.

We've inadvertently trained our kids to only really pay attention once we've said it a few times or have begun shouting.

To gain better cooperation with your child you're going to have to change your own behaviour first.

Gulp. This was a hard pill for me to swallow too.

We want to blame them and make them be the ones to change, but the change begins with us.

We need to stop taking it personally when they ignore us and that's easier to do when you accept that it's not about *you*. Kids need to learn how to act and the best way to teach them is by example, not getting mad at them.

Has your child ever wanted your attention and you've said, 'Yeah, in a minute' and then a minute goes by and you're annoyed that they've already asked again? We expect them to listen to us, but not vice versa.

Here's how to get your child to listen to you the first time you say it:

1. Sit down and have a chat.

Lovingly explain that you're no longer going to shout or repeat and from now on when you ask them to do something, they'll need to do it. Without blaming them, try to describe how you feel when they don't listen. Tell them how happy you'll feel when you don't have to repeat or shout to be heard.

2. Write it down as a rule.

When it's written down you can point to the rule, rather than saying it all over again. Reward them with positive feedback each time they cooperate. Remember that the rule applies to you too. Just as you're expecting your child to form a new habit of listening to you, it will be challenging for you to form a new habit in the way that you give instructions. (See steps 3 and 4.) You'll also need to model the behaviour you want to see by listening to them when they need you. It's a two-way deal.

3. Give your instruction in a firm but warm tone.

Don't reserve your most sarcastic, exasperated, shouty voice for your family. When you use a nice tone you'll not only get better cooperation, but you'll also feel better doing it.

4. Get into their space.

If you're in the habit of barking orders from one room to another, this will be a new challenge for you, but worth the effort. Go to them. Engage them. Get them to look at you. Have them repeat the request back to you.

'Olivia, what have I asked you to do now?'

'Stop playing and get undressed for my bath?'

'Yes. Thank you for listening to me the first time. See you in the bathroom!'

5. See it from your child's point of view.

This is not a dictatorship where your child must always drop whatever they're doing the second you say it.

It's hard to validate that your child feels it's just as important to finish his video game as you feel it's important he comes to eat the meal you've prepared. But imagine if you were in the middle of your favourite TV series and your partner suddenly burst in and ordered you to look at some tax papers NOW. Would you immediately switch it off and gleefully skip to the next room with them? Or would you feel annoyed?

So, knowing that dinner is nearly ready, give your child the heads up that in five minutes he'll need to come to the table.

Don't shout this out from the kitchen. Stop what you're doing and go to them. Make eye contact and tell him in person. If your child is engrossed in something, take a moment before giving your instruction to engage with him about what he's doing.

'What are you watching, Jake?'

'This really cool show about cars.'

'Wow, that really does look cool. Look at that red one! Now Jake, look at me for a minute. Thank you. In five minutes your dinner is ready. You can press pause on that if you want and then you need to wash your hands straight away and come to the table.'

'OK.'

'What do you need to do now?'

'Pause this and wash my hands.'

'Good, yes. And then come to the table. Thanks for listening, Jake. See you at the table in five!'

It may feel like it will take a long time to stop what you're doing, go to your child, engage them, give the instruction and have it repeated back – but let's compare this to shouting the instruction from another room several times.

By the time he comes to the table you're peeved that you had to repeat and yell, he's upset that he had to stop watching his show and now everyone's in a bad mood. He might play up during his meal and then you have yet *another* battle on your hands.

By taking just a minute to give the instruction politely, in person, you'll both feel happier and more relaxed.

Always remember to give positive feedback *every* time they listen to you the first time: 'I really love how you came to the table the first time I asked you. Thank you!'

If you find yourself slipping back into repeating yourself, start over again.

Remember, it takes time to establish new habits. If you or your child slip up, take a deep breath, see it as a mistake, be forgiving – then try, try again!

Whenever I'm complimented on how well my boys listen to me, I think back to how things used to be. It isn't always easy and we still have our moments, but I wouldn't go back to the way things were for anything.

Rules RULE!

Having clear, written expectations (i.e. rules!) has helped me more than I can possibly say. If you only kind of know what you want to happen and your kids only kind of know what they ought to be doing, it's a recipe for chaos.

Limits actually give them a sense of security. And kids raised in a safe, secure and predictable environment are known to have higher self-esteem, resist peer pressure and make better judgements.

If you want your kids to behave well at home and school, with friends and with relatives, and to stay out of trouble, you need to set boundaries. Get clear about your expectations, set limits and convey them to your kids in a calm, positive way.

Whenever I notice that my kids need constant reminding about something, I know I need to create a written rule around it. Once it's established and enforced consistently, it becomes a habit. I haven't had to remind my boys to hang up a wet towel in years. I made a rule for it when they were always leaving towels on the floor and over time it became a good habit to hang them up.

This is what making rules is really about. **Creating good habits.** If you view it this way, you'll be more compassionate when your children slip up. Think of how **you** feel when you fall back into old bad habits. Compassion does not equal complacence: it just means you'll gently remind them and follow through until they get it right.

Although it can be tough being the enforcer, it shows you care about your kids. When groups of young adults were interviewed about their childhoods, many wished their parents had made *more* limits and been stricter. They perceived that their peers, who'd grown up with clear rules, had parents who cared more. They also felt they would have done better if there had been more routines and discipline.

Parents who are consistent have an easier time than parents who aren't specific or are too flexible. Saying 'no' isn't always easy. You cave in to avoid the immediate reaction, but if you don't deal with poor behaviour now, you're setting yourself up for bigger trouble later. If you've established good habits when they're younger, think of how much easier it'll be when they're hormonal teenagers.

It's never too late to start!

Here's how to make rules for kids:

1. Identify the hotspots.

Over the next few days, simply observe. Where do the biggest or most frequent problems occur? Write these down and think about which rules would help. Common areas include: mealtimes, bedtime, homework, technology, tidying up, siblings, hygiene, dressing.

2. Create written expectations.

For younger children, draw stick figures, print a photo off the internet or take a photo of your child actually *doing* the right thing. For older children, write them in a positive way. Instead of 'No fighting in the bath', reverse it to say 'Play nicely in the bath'. Start with just a few rules. You can add more once you begin to experience some small successes.

3. Call a family meeting.

Rules shouldn't be dished out in a stern, punitive manner. Serve some snacks and make it a light-hearted occasion. Explain that you want to make some positive changes for the whole family to make the house feel happier. Give examples. What does 'Nice table manners' mean exactly? Break it all down into clear, small steps and confirm that they understand. If you find resistance, practise empathy and patience.

4. Give positive feedback.

If you're used to only giving your energy to what's going wrong, turn this around.

Start noticing everything they get right. Actively look for the good. Tell them you've noticed the effort they're making, thank them for remembering the rule, smile more, hug a lot. Get excited about any steps they make in the right direction.

5. **Follow through and be consistent.**

   If they get away with it one day because you're too preoccupied or tired to enforce it, then the rule is worthless. You'll be starting all over again, dragging out the whole process of 'rule into habit'. When your child misbehaves, respond in a calm, flat tone. Remind them of the rule and follow through.

breathe in

I DO MY BEST

breathe out

**I LET GO
OF THE REST**

How to Stop Sibling Squabbles

Are you sick of hearing your kids bicker? When my boys were three and six I was at my wits' end. They were constantly fighting. My older son played the good cop and felt it was his duty to stop his younger brother from doing anything 'naughty'. 'No no, no no!' was his continuous catch phrase. Of course, this only fuelled the little one's fire and he quickly became the rebel, doing everything *except* what he was supposed to.

Even short car journeys were a nightmare, with each one pointing to something they saw out of their side of the window. If one of them had more interesting things on *their* side, the other would have a fit. I started taking back roads just to avoid construction sites, as bulldozers were the ultimate prize and I knew it would cause tears.

It was a downward spiral and I felt utterly exasperated. Their complete inability to get along for more than five minutes was driving me crazy.

I decided this issue needed some focused attention and figuring out on paper. Once I put my mind to it, I managed to turn things around. I implemented a few of the things I'd learned in my parenting skills course and combined it with some reflections on not getting along with my own brother as a kid.

Within a few months my boys went from fighting 90 per cent of the time to less than 10 per cent. What a turnaround! I smile now when people comment on what good friends they are.

So how did they go from foes to friends?

Good question and one I have to break down into steps, as it didn't happen overnight.

1. **Give positive feedback.**

   I began noticing when they *weren't* fighting. When they played for even two minutes without a squabble, I'd say something like, 'Wow, I love seeing you two playing so nicely!' with a huge smile on my face. When driving I'd say it was 'music to my ears' to be in a peaceful car and thank them for being so quiet. When one did something kind for the other, I made sure they noticed I'd noticed! By giving more attention to the good than the bad, things definitely improved.

2. **Avoid competitiveness and comparison.**

   No more saying things like, 'Who can get dressed first?' or 'Why don't you finish your dinner like your brother?' I encouraged my husband to stop making them race against each other when we were out for walks. We made a point of looking at schoolwork and report cards with each one separately and never comparing their grades or abilities in anything.

3. **Spend 'one-on-one' time with each of them.**

   This isn't always easy, but filling their love tanks daily makes a big difference. I made a real effort to connect with them individually by reading meaningful books together and playing games like the ones I've listed in the Family resources section (see page 283). These are great tools to spark lively conversations and they help with self-esteem, emotional literacy and understanding values.

4. **Promote sibling love.**

   I commented on how lucky they were to have a brother to play with. I didn't expect a response; it was just something I sprinkled into the mix every so often.

   After a few months, a real friendship evolved. The spats became few and far between and they began to genuinely enjoy spending time together. Even now they make a great double act.

If sibling squabbles are driving you bonkers, take the bull by the horns and do something about it. The longer you wait, the more time you're wasting. Yes, they might grow out of it – or not. Is that a risk you're willing to take?

I do ALL things with a loving heart.

www.myprojectme.com

Giving Positive Feedback

When children feel good about themselves, it sets them up for success. They take pride in their abilities, take on new challenges, cope with mistakes and try their best. They are less likely to succumb to peer pressure, are less hard on themselves, and they feel more confident and valued. They also behave better.

I hear mixed messages about praising children. Logic tells me that it's a good idea to let my kids know when I'm happy about something they've done well, yet some parenting experts say we damage our kids when we constantly shower them with praise. They'll come to rely on our approval and will only behave well if we're noticing.

When I began using 'descriptive praise', after learning about it my Parent Practice course, there was a dramatic improvement in my children's behaviour. I'd fallen into the bad habit of only noticing when they were doing something wrong. 'Stop doing that!' 'Leave him alone!' 'Get back in your chair and eat!' I couldn't stand the sound of my own voice.

Then I learned to pay more attention to when they were getting it right. In the beginning, there wasn't a whole lot, but I looked hard for the little things and gave positive feedback to simply describe what I was seeing. 'You stayed sitting in your chair for one whole minute!' (In a happy, cheerful voice.) 'You two are working on that project together. What a great team you make!' (When they'd only been playing Lego for two minutes and neither had crashed down the other's creation yet.)

I learned that 'Good boy/girl!' isn't specific enough and is too evaluative. 'You're so clever!' is inflated praise that they either discount as false or it puts too much pressure on them to keep pleasing you in this way. It can be hard to know what to say when you open your mouth after a while! I eventually learned to relax into it and try to remember these three points:

- Say more positive things than criticisms.
- Let them know when they're doing well by describing what you see.
- Use a more friendly tone overall.

> I contacted Kelly to tackle the Work area in my life but soon realised (after shedding some tears!) that the Family area really needed some attention and was in a state of disarray. My life was completely ruled by my three children! I was brought up in a big, noisy, boisterous family with a harassed, stressed-out mother and felt that history was repeating itself.
>
> With Kelly's guidance and support, I started with scheduling a block of time each week to complete an online parenting course with The Parent Practice. I turned up at my online course every Thursday morning as if I was attending the course in person. Just feeling that I was doing something positive already helped my mindset. I really enjoyed taking the time to do the course and I'm still implementing the recommendations. It's an ongoing process.
>
> I've changed the way I talk to my children – less blaming, more descriptive praise and empathy. I've put more structure in place and become more consistent with bedtime and schoolwork, music practice and electronics. It helps my children to know where they stand.
>
> I've started meditating every day and it's made me much more aware of how I'm behaving in front of my children and helps me to regulate my emotions. I've also accepted that the children will behave like children and to be more realistic in my expectations!
>
> I'm prioritising my own exercise, whereas before I focused only on the children doing exercise, and we're all eating much more healthily. Sugary snacks are kept for the weekend and occasional treats.
>
> It's still early days and we have good days and bad; however, I feel we're moving in the right direction. Now whenever I'm starting to get upset, my nine-year-old son rushes to give me a hug and tells me to take deep breaths. I feel it's all worth it!
>
> **–Catriona**

Building Close Communication

I've learned that being a peaceful parent isn't just about learning to manage my emotions; it's also about fostering a deep connection with my kids. It's important that they know they can talk to me about anything. I never felt that way growing up. It's sad to read my old diaries from age ten to eighteen. I lied about what I was doing and whom I was doing it with. I didn't feel I had anyone I could talk to about mean girls at school and my insecurities and worries. I don't want my own kids to feel that way, so I've always been an open book with them. I share how I'm feeling, the ups and downs of my day and stories of my childhood, so they realise I was once a kid too and I remember what it was like.

I've told them to preface tricky conversations with: 'I want to tell you something but I don't want you to get mad', which gives me a chance to take a deep breath and listen *without getting mad*. And they seem to tell me what's going on in their lives.

A good relationship with your child gets you through the hard times and creates more good times. The more tuned-in you are with your child, the more you'll notice the signs if something's wrong. Children who feel a special connection with their parents are more likely to see them as being on their side rather than against them.

My top three tips for building close communication with your child

1. Truly listen.

Listening builds trust. The more your child feels they can talk to you about anything, the better. If a child feels cut-off too often or afraid to ask questions, the chances of them opening up to you later will be slim.

Keep the door to communication wide open now so when they become teenagers (and the door naturally closes more), there'll still be a crack left open for you to get inside.

Show interest when your child speaks to you. This means looking up from whatever you're doing and making eye contact. Older children and teens are particularly put off talking when they don't feel they have your full attention.

2. Ask questions and share.

Show your child you care about what's happening in their life. Ask questions that require more than a one-word response. 'How was your day?' is only going to elicit a one-word answer. 'Who did you play with today?' or 'How was that science test? Was it as hard as you thought it would be?' give more scope for a real conversation. Don't ask the same questions every day.

Share about your own day. Our kids are in their own world and don't usually think about what we've been up to. The more we share how we're feeling, the more we're modelling it for them.

Be open to what they say. Press pause on your reaction if you don't like what you hear. Don't turn every conversation into a lecture. Resist pushing or prodding for information.

If you're overly involved in solving their problems for them or turning small things into big issues, they might not come to you if they're facing peer pressure or are in trouble. They need to trust that you won't steam in and make things worse.

3. Be available.

As your child grows older and homework, friendships and extracurricular activities take over, you may need to work harder at finding time to connect. Notice times when your child is more likely to talk – at bedtime, in the car or sharing an after-school snack.

Make regular time for one-on-one activities with your child, even if it's simply running a few errands together. These small moments of 'special time' help build a bond between you and they're less likely to act out negatively for attention.

Project Me Mama Mantra:

I AM A PRO PROBLEM SOLVER!

www.myprojectme.com

Taming Technology

Raising kids in this digital age is hard. This degree of technology simply didn't exist when we were growing up and we don't have any definitive guidance for how to handle it. Our kids are the guinea pigs and only time will reveal if we 'should' have been doing things differently.

My kids probably spend too much time on technology – as do I. But we've stuck quite firmly to a rule of 'no technology at meals'. It makes me sad to see entire families glued to their phones in restaurants – nobody speaking to each other or, even worse, a child wearing headphones and watching a film as the parents converse.

If we let our kids have unlimited screen time and pull out a phone every time they're bored, what are *they* going to be like as parents? The next generation won't even feel guilty about it the way we do. It's up to us to teach them how to play cards and board games and show them 'old-fashioned' ways to combat boredom and have fun.

Dr Kristy Goodwin is an expert on the impact of technology on children. She's also a mother herself and knows the answer isn't banning iPads or disconnecting the internet. She says:

> As parents we're often given conflicting and inaccurate advice when it comes to screens and kids. On one hand we're told that our children need to be proficient with technology so they're not 'left behind' in this digital world. On the other hand, we're told that screens are detrimental to children's development and should be avoided at all costs.
>
> It's not about fearing or ignoring the use of it, but we need to teach children how to use technology in healthy and helpful ways to minimise some of its potentially harmful effects. We want to arm them with strategies so they can manage technology and not the other way around where technology manages them.

If you want to gain a better sense of control over technology in your family, use a Challenge Solver Action Sheet to outline your specific concerns, then brainstorm some solutions. See the Family resources section (page 283) for extra guidance.

Take Action!

Use a Challenge Solver Action Sheet to identify any particular hotspots in the Family area of your life. Don't try to figure this out in your head. Writing it down will help you get clarity over what the challenge is. If you aren't sure what the solution is, head to the Family resources section at the end of this book. With a little digging, you'll unearth your answers.

Most ideas need breaking down into step-by-step actions. An Ideas Into Action Sheet will help you do this.

All Project Me Action Sheets can be found at www.myprojectme.com/action-sheets.

health

Health and Wellbeing

Your health is arguably the most important petal on your Life Wheel. If you're suffering poor health, it affects all of the other areas too. Likewise, if you're vibrantly healthy in mind and body it makes challenges in other areas of your life easier to move through.

Self-care is an act of generosity to your entire family. Nurturing your soul and body is a must if you want to offer your best self to the people you interact with every day. You can't give what you haven't got!

If you run around non-stop every day, eat junk, feel stressed or don't get enough sleep – you'll run out of battery. And before that even happens, the warning signs will be there. Snappy, irritable, moody, low-energy, lacking motivation: rather than thinking these are part of your personality, dig behind them and find the cause. I used to label myself as wildly impatient and beat myself up for how explosive I was with my kids and husband. I'd never describe myself like this now. The more I get to know myself and what brings out my best and worst, the more I realise that I need to nurture myself daily in small ways.

Some of the most important ways I nurture my health and wellbeing are:

- Good sleep
- Breathing, meditation, mindfulness
- Fitness and movement
- Healthy eating
- Mama Me Time

Nearly half of the mothers in my Project Me Health survey said they don't nurture themselves as much as they need or want to. I asked them: What stops you from nurturing and caring for yourself more? What do you think you could do differently or more of? These were some of the answers:

I feel guilty and I have a hard time asking others for help. If I let that anxiety go, it would take a lot of pressure off.
I need to say no to more things.
I should go to bed earlier.
I fall into negative patterns of checking social media rather than actively doing something more positive that shifts my thoughts, such as meditation or yoga.
Lack of willpower. I'd feel so much better if I lost some weight.

Need to drink less wine – it's a bad habit to have wine at night and one I keep resolving to break but never do anything about.

The most common reason given is lack of time. If this is you, interweave what you learn in this section with some strategies in the Productivity chapter so you can make more space in your life for it.

The other common excuse is the guilt of doing something for ourselves. We've all heard about putting your own oxygen mask on first or you won't be able to help your child with theirs, yet too many of us are doing it backwards. We think we're being selfish if we do something for ourselves. The truth is, the list of things you could be doing around the home for your family is never-ending. If you think you're going to get to the bottom of that list and then start doing something for you, it'll never happen. Self-denial may sound noble, but it leads to anger and resentment, and often to illness. Start to put yourself closer to the top of that long list so when you're prioritising your to-dos, you don't continue to fall to the bottom of the heap. You'll be of no use to anyone if you don't take care of yourself.

There are many potential reasons for marking yourself low in the Health area of your life. Maybe you're not happy with how you look on the outside – weight, skin, hair. Or your body is struggling on the inside by giving you symptoms like poor digestion, bad circulation, aches and pains. You may have a doctor telling you that you *must* make some changes. Your emotions and energy levels are also a signal that things are not well on the inside. Low mood, irritability and lack of motivation are common examples. Depression and mental illness are now often treated with a focus on diet and nutrition.

Begin to really listen to your body, paying more attention to what it's trying to tell you.

> I've been listening to my body better over the last couple of years and have made many changes (dietary, hormonal, exercise). As a result, I feel better than I have in years. I'm even training for my first full marathon, something I never thought I would be able to do. Every once in a while, I forget to listen, but when I start feeling bad again, it's a good reminder to listen to my body!
> **—Stacey, mother of seven**

Don't wait until you're forced into action. It's too easy to bury your head in the sand and hope things will get better on their own. Educate yourself on things relating to your own specific health concerns, then come up with a small-step action plan to start to move yourself forward.

It's easy to ignore health niggles. They become so normal that you become desensitised to them, including the negative effects of stress. Have you heard that if a frog is placed in a pan of boiling water it'll jump out quickly, yet when it's placed in cool water with the heat turned up gradually, it won't realise the danger and will stay in the pan and boil to death? Think about this analogy in relation to your own life. Are you so used to running around, juggling balls and spinning plates that stress or anxiety has become your new normal? Are you ignoring the danger signs instead of jumping out of that hot pan? Living on the edge sends huge amounts of cortisol zooming around the body – not a good thing. Too much cortisol depletes your immune system, affects your sleep, gives you unhealthy food cravings, lowers your sex drive and makes you feel like crap. You're far more likely to flip your lid over any and *every*thing, let small things get you down and lose your ability to think straight or remember anything.

Doing my 'me-search'

It's taken me a while to get to the place where I notice the heat when it's getting too warm. I'm now so used to feeling *good* that as soon as I get a tightness in my chest, pang in my stomach or feel hot-headed, I think, 'Whoa! What's going on here?' The old me would have ignored the warning signals and carried on. The new me hits pause and does some **me**-search. I ask myself, 'What's wrong? Why am I feeling this way?'

If I'm overwhelmed, I whip out a Magic Matrix Action Sheet (see page 81). Once I've got my to-do list onto the grid, I have a clear picture of what really needs doing **now** and what can wait. It clears up mental headspace fast. Try it for yourself.

When I'm feeling anxious or pondering a decision, I know I need to get it out of my head and onto paper. I grab a Challenge Solver Action Sheet (see page 34) and find a solution. I no longer ignore it or think I'll deal with it when I'm 'less busy'.

If I'm snapping at my kids or husband, I know I need to feed myself with some patience-inducing self-care, like getting to bed earlier, eating healthier, allowing myself to relax and drop perfection. An evening bubble bath while listening to a guided meditation followed by reading a chapter in an inspirational book is one of my greatest gifts to myself. The power of immersing yourself in positivity is not to be underestimated.

I no longer live with problems or worries long enough that they become my *new normal*. I recognise when something's up and take action to do something about it. I gently urge you to become the expert of you. Learn to listen to your inner guidance system. Recognise the signals that something's not right.

Here's a story from back in the days when I didn't know how to listen to my body:

I used to live with constipation and bloating because I simply didn't know anything different. My saviour came in the form of a naturopath named Max Tomlinson. He was testing out a new detox plan and I volunteered to be a guinea pig. As I was considering trying for a baby, it seemed sensible to have a good clear-out before conceiving.

Max asked me a lot of questions about my health and diet and was not happy to hear that my bowel movements were extremely infrequent, often several days in between. Some days I could do up my jeans, other days it was impossible. I'd always had a silly phobia about pooing in public, which meant I didn't go at work all day. He couldn't believe I accepted this as normal. He told me I'd been ignoring the signal of an oncoming bowel movement for so long that my brain no longer registered it. From now on I'd need to listen for that signal, stop anything I was doing and go. I explained about my busy job, the crazy deadlines and ringing phones. Max looked me in the eye and told me I was literally full of shit. 'Everybody poos. Get over it,' he ordered. From that day forward I've taken his advice and I pay attention to that signal. Even if it means I'll be a little bit late. Even if it means going at someone else's house or in a cubicle with someone next to me. When I gotta go, I go. I have amazing digestion now. Best advice ever.

In addition, Max woke me up to the vast amount of wheat, dairy and processed foods I was consuming every day. He advised me to read all food labels and never buy anything I couldn't make myself at home with those same ingredients. I took his advice, my tummy went flat and I could wear what I liked every day! My energy levels soared and my frequent headaches disappeared. No crazy strict diet, just some tweaks. Some other problems I'd previously accepted as 'normal' disappeared too. For years I'd been using feminine and foot odour sprays. I see these products now in the shops and I cringe to think of how much money I was spending to mask the problem of being so full of shit that it was leaching out of my body.

I can still be found today in the supermarket aisles, squinting at the ingredient labels and putting stuff back. Max's advice truly improved my health. I conceived my first son a few weeks after my detox and I even named him . . . Max!

Whether your motivation for wanting to eat healthier or exercise more is primarily about looking good on the outside, or you're looking to improve your health on the inside, the fact is it works both ways. Shedding excess weight and improving your diet not only helps you to look better in your clothes (and naked), it also lowers your risk of high blood pressure, heart disease, stroke, type 2 diabetes, back and joint pain and some types of cancer. Even 5–10 per cent weight loss can noticeably improve your sleep, energy and vitality. Making small, realistic changes to your diet and how physically active you are will make a positive difference to your health. Remember that your ideal weight is the weight that *feels* good for you – in your head and in your heart.

If you're past the niggly symptom stage and you're here because you need to make some serious changes right away, seek professional advice and **take action** on it.

Health Check-Ups and Screenings

Regular check-ups are the best way to spot any health issues early on. It's not fun to think about there being anything seriously wrong with you, but far better to catch it now and treat it. Prevention is better than cure. Health checks might include:

- Cervical smear tests
- Blood pressure tests
- Cholesterol level checks
- Body mass index (BMI) and obesity tests
- Diabetes checks

If you have any more specific health concerns, then your doctor will be able to advise you on these and conduct the proper checks. It's also advised to check your breasts regularly for lumps and changes as well as studying your skin for changes in moles or freckles. If you notice anything unusual, schedule a doctor's appointment. I'm happy I had a doctor check out a funny mole on my arm that kept changing colour. It turned out to be cancerous and it was cut out in a simple procedure. I have friends with similar success stories over moles and lumps that were caught in time to be treated. Don't ignore these things.

In my Project Me Health survey I asked women if they were up to date with their screenings and check-ups. 70 per cent reported they were – 30 per cent thanked me for the nudge. Here's your friendly nudge if you need it!

Healthy Eating

I'm not one for diets or fads and my dyscalculia (it's like dyslexia but with numbers) is so bad I couldn't even begin to count calories or work out an 80:20 diet. Instead I adopt a 'healthy-enough' approach, which means I cook mostly from fresh, natural ingredients but will throw a frozen pizza in the oven occasionally and not feel bad about it. I happen to love fruits and vegetables and don't have much of a sweet tooth, so I'm not fighting anything other than a resistance to spending a lot of time in the kitchen. I'm not great at winging it and really need a recipe to follow – the easier the better. Meal planning is my saviour and I share my meal planning tips and Weekly Meal Planner in the Productivity section (see page 92).

Emotional eating

I remember the evenings I used to spend on the sofa, watching TV and trying to stop myself from getting up and going to the kitchen to get something more to eat. I now understand it as emotional eating – the emotion being **boredom**. My life is so hugely fulfilling now that the craving to eat something more after dinner simply isn't there any more. It's as if I'm filled up with a bigger purpose instead of more food.

TV hypnotist Paul McKenna writes about emotional eating in his book *I Can Make You Thin*. He says the number one reason people eat when they're not hungry is to cover up a negative emotion or to fill an emotional hole.

I really like his non-diet approach of eating only when we're hungry and stopping when we're full. To stop myself from grazing on the kids' uneaten dinner scraps, I used to take the spray bottle of disinfectant to the table when I was clearing up and spray their plates. That way I'd scrape it into the bin without shovelling any into my mouth first. *Give up your membership to the Clean Plate Club and stop treating yourself like the rubbish bin!*

Healthy eating is a huge struggle that takes up a lot of headspace for many women. Food cravings, food restrictions due to allergies, health conditions, hormonal imbalances, IBS – I hear from mothers who really suffer when it comes to food and eating. Don't bury your head in the sand. Educate yourself.

Be the expert of you.

> *I've realised that a big part of maintaining good health is about knowing myself: how much sleep I need, what foods make me feel good, how I can create healthy habits that last long-term, understanding that I need alone time to re-energise, etc., and then being true to these. What works for others might not always work for me, and I need to advocate for myself to ensure that my individual needs are met along with those of other members in my family.*
> **—Becs**

Drink more water!

We all know we need to be drinking a lot more water. It increases energy levels, relieves fatigue, improves skin complexion, boosts the immune system, relieves and prevents headaches, aids digestion, reduces hunger and puts you in a good mood by giving you an overall better-functioning body. The image that sticks in my mind the most is that when we don't drink enough water, we aren't flushing out toxins so they stay stuck in our body. Yuck! Isn't that motivation enough to glug down some water right now? *Go ahead, I'll wait.*

Hey beautiful mama, drink some water.

#WATERBREAK

Physical Fitness

Are you getting enough exercise? Aside from the obvious benefit of looking in good physical shape, there are other solid reasons to keep moving your body:

- It makes you stronger, which gives you more energy. You can move heavy stuff around, carry more shopping bags, reach for that top shelf and, most importantly, keep up with your kids. You aren't so knackered all of the time. Being stronger and leaner makes you more capable, which makes life more manageable. Everything doesn't feel like such a hard slog.
- It improves your mood. When you exercise, your body releases endorphins which then trigger a positive feeling in the body, similar to morphine! This gives you an overall more positive outlook on life.
- It gives you a fresh perspective. When you exercise it refocuses your attention from your daily problems to the workout itself. When you're finished and return to your normal daily tasks, you approach them with a better attitude and some new ways to figure things out.
- It boosts memory, builds intelligence and reduces the risk of dementia. Regular exercise is shown to help keep your neurons in shape, send more oxygen to the brain and improve the flow of blood through your body. Not only will this help you to be less forgetful now, but do it for your future self too. Keep that brain sharp!

Before I became a mother I had no fitness routine. I didn't have a gym membership and I didn't run or do any sport. When I wasn't working I was socialising and I pretty much took my health for granted.

After I had my first baby I heard that my local gym offered a crèche service for members. You could drop your little one off for up to an hour and a half! I saw this as an opportunity for Me Time to work out, do some fun classes, go swimming and (this was the best bit) have a shower, wash, condition and blow-dry my hair in peace. I could even squeeze in a visit to the juice bar and chat to some of my new mama gym buddies. Bliss. Yes, in the beginning my son often screamed when he saw me leaving and I'd end up checking through the glass every few minutes with my stomach in knots. But I'm glad I persevered because it was a win-win situation. He learned how to have adventures and play with other children without me hovering over him; I got some much-needed time to myself and a fitter body than I'd ever had. It made my son's transition into nursery school easier too. We'd got the separation anxiety out of the way much earlier.

Find your fitness groove

Have you fallen out of the fitness groove and need some inspiration to get you moving again? Finding a workout that's fun and fits in with your schedule can be a challenge, but it's one worth overcoming.

The very first step is to figure out what you enjoy doing – you're not going to stick at it if you're doing it through gritted teeth. Find the workout that works for *you* and get those feel-good endorphins flowing through your veins.

Here are a few ideas to get you thinking about what might work for you:

- Hit the gym. The great thing about a gym is the variety on offer. The bad part is the expense, especially if you don't use it. If you've got a gym membership, get on down there and have a look at the class list. Zumba, barre, spinning, aqua-fit, boxing . . . be open to trying anything – you might surprise yourself. Alternate days so you also use the cardio machines and weight equipment. If you're not sure how something works, get an instructor to show you. You're paying for membership – so either use it, or drop it.
- Use the great outdoors. Find a local boot camp, sign up for tennis lessons, go for a brisk walk or run. An outdoor workout gives you lots of bang for your buck. The smells and sounds of nature will switch off that internal chatter, plus you get your all-important dose of vitamin D – the sunshine vitamin.
- Work out at home. If getting out of the house isn't an option, try one of the live

and interactive online classes listed in the Health resources (see page 285). There are classes for all levels at times to suit your schedule.

- Exercise with the kids. Play hide and seek, tag, skip, dance, kick a ball around, throw a frisbee. Instead of idly watching your child at the playground, go a little crazy with some tricep dips, a run around the perimeter of the fence, and some pull-ups. If you've got a baby, sign up for buggyfit classes so you can exercise in the park with your child, get fit and make friends all at once. Playing with the kids makes you feel like a kid and gives you a great opportunity to connect and have fun together.
- Do it with a friend. Accountability is king – it's too easy to opt out if you're on your own. You need a *really* good excuse to let a friend down.
- Reframe housework as a workout! Put on some of your favourite dance tunes. Exaggerate the moves as you squat down to clean low surfaces and reach up to get to high places. Eighties-style headband and leg warmers optional.
- Mix in some yoga. Some classes are spiritual; others are more of a workout. Even the more hard-core classes end with a few minutes of lying on your back, eyes closed and breathing – a blissful and well-deserved treat for any busy mother. Yoga is also an investment in your long-term flexibility. You'll be able to get out of a chair without assistance in your old age.

I EAT LIKE I LOVE MYSELF.

I MOVE LIKE I LOVE MYSELF.

I SPEAK LIKE I LOVE MYSELF.

I ACT LIKE I LOVE MYSELF.

#ProjectMe

Lack of time – and motivation

Many mothers have serious time challenges. Sometimes it's a bad combo of lack of time and low motivation, like for these mothers who took the Project Me Health survey:

> *Whether I'm at work or home or out, there are always SO many distractions. People mostly – kid, spouse, pets, co-workers, friends, acquaintances. Someone always wants my time spent on them. But things are also distracting – dirty dishes, dirty clothes, clean clothes not yet put away, toys and gadgets that don't belong to me. I almost always want to hide under the covers.*
> **–Amanda**
>
> *I'm a single mom with three kids and I'm currently working two jobs. I always put their needs first. When I do have time away from them, I tend to go out with my friends and drink too much. I need to find a different way to decompress.*
> **–Marie**
>
> *Lack of exercise is partly because I don't get much time to myself, but also due to lack of motivation when I actually do have the time, as by then energy levels can be lagging!*
> **–Sue**

Pep talk!

Mama, I'm here to give you a motivational pep talk to make your health a priority. Do you really want to wait until you have a serious health scare to force you into making changes? Do you understand that unless you get proactive about your health, you're not in control of your life? Can you see the negative knock-on effect your low Health score is having on other areas of your life? Where can you let go of perfection in other areas to free up a little more time? Your family need you to be healthy and alive more than anything else.

Identify some poor habits that aren't serving you. How can you step out of your comfort zone and do things differently? Yes, it feels overwhelming to think about a complete diet and exercise overhaul, so don't go there. Baby steps are all you need.

It's important to see the correlation between lack of energy and not getting enough physical movement. It's hard to muster up the energy to make a game plan when you're in this state of mind and body. Recognise this and don't wait until you have a magical surge of vitality to get started. It may never happen.

Here's how I helped one time-strapped mama to improve her health and fitness. Maria scored herself low in the Health area of her Life Wheel. Juggling two kids and two jobs meant no time to exercise, so she'd thought it was impossible to improve this area of her life.

I got her to write down her Dream Vision of herself looking and feeling fit, healthy, energised and glowing. She loved this exercise and went on to brainstorm some small ideas of what she could manage to do towards her health:

- *Put all my cut-out recipes in a ring binder for easier and quicker access.*
- *Set aside time in the morning to make myself a healthy snack to take when I'm working my second job.*
- *Go on a thirty-minute run on Saturdays.*

By choosing some small, easy-to-do small-step actions, Maria was able to get off the starting blocks easily. Already after the first week she had more energy and motivation. After four weeks she said:

> *It's reaffirmed my belief in wanting to be fit and healthy but more importantly to stay fit and healthy. It's brought a more positive me. I'm much more organised and in control. It's helped me to start working on other areas of my life.*
>
> The simple act of taking a few small steps in one life area can really get the ball rolling in other areas too. It's all about getting off the starting blocks instead of waiting until you have more time or have an entire long-term game plan figured out.

Ditch the 'all or nothing' attitude

Are you the type of person who wants to do it all perfectly, or not at all? If something gets in the way of your workouts one week (or you pig out over the weekend), do you throw in the towel on your goal? 'All or nothing' thinking is a big block to making positive changes.

Things happen. Stuff gets in the way. You flake out.

Practise forgiveness. Don't beat yourself up. Jump back in the saddle again as soon as you're able. If you're prone to having an 'all or nothing' mindset, whether it be about fitness or anything else, swap it for: 'A little bit or nothing'.

If you can't work out for a whole hour, what if you dropped down to the floor and did twenty sit-ups, then flipped over and did however many push-ups you can do, then stood up and did twenty squats and twenty lunges? This is what I do when I'm on holiday and I'm feeling hot and lazy. I tell myself I just need to do twenty of each of those things as a minimum and that's good enough. No need to change into workout gear!

If you're an 'all or nothing' type with food, you might be better off having none at all if having even one mouthful means you can't stop. If you know yourself and you can have just a little and then not feel deprived and miserable, go ahead. Once you become the expert of yourself you'll know how to play it.

Schedule fitness into your week

I know by now that if my fitness is not scheduled in, something else will always get in the way. I created a **Weekly Fitness Planner** chart to write down my overarching fitness goal and then my micro goal for the week. I need a lot of variety to keep me interested and motivated. Just like meal planning, I sit down on a Sunday and plot out how I'm going to move my body in the week ahead. When the day comes, I treat it like an important doctor's appointment (because it is that important) and I don't cancel on myself. When it's inked into the Fitness Planner, it's a done deal. It's about making a commitment to my health and honouring it.

I'm sharing my Weekly Fitness Planner with you so you'll have the same tool I use. *Take action!*

Journal Prompt

- ★ Why would I like to eat better or move my body more? What are the benefits?
- ★ What stops me from eating better or moving my body more?
- ★ Which of these reasons are valid – and which might be excuses?
- ★ What will happen if I do nothing?
- ★ What ideas do I have to improve things?
- ★ What are three small steps I can take this week towards improving my health?

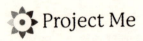

Project Me

Date .... / .... / ....

★ Weekly Fitness Planner ★

My big burning goal: ....

My goal this week: ....

☐ MONDAY

☐ TUESDAY

☐ WEDNESDAY

☐ THURSDAY

☐ FRIDAY

☐ SATURDAY

☐ SUNDAY

HOW DID I DO?

Remember to plan for next week. If it's not scheduled, it's not happening!

move!

I COMMIT

TO GET FIT!

www.myprojectme.com

Mental Fitness

A healthy mind is every bit as important as a healthy body. Your mental wellbeing sets the stage for how well you can perform in your day-to-day life and influences your levels of happiness as you go about it.

If you're constantly worrying, feeling anxious, stressed, overwhelmed, angry or resentful and you're unable to channel these emotions in a healthy way, your body is spending way too much time dealing with this rather than your normal bodily functions and, guess what? You'll end up depleted – and then sick. Or with aches and pains and all kinds of other physical problems that stemmed from your state of mind.

59 per cent of the mothers I surveyed said they regularly feel stressed. If you feel the same way, you need to start paying attention to your stress triggers. Could you be doing anything differently to reduce feeling triggered? The very act of working on your Project Me means greater awareness of the things in your life that aren't working. It also means you have emotional tools for dealing with the things you can't change.

Keeping a healthy mind isn't always easy, but there are ways to keep mentally fit and get yourself out of negative thought patterns. Let's begin to explore some of those now.

Sleep, Glorious Sleep!

Quality sleep is **the** number one way to feel better physically and emotionally. We all need varying amounts of sleep to wake up feeling 100 per cent, ranging from seven to nine hours a night. There is a rare one per cent of people who can honestly get by with less than that, so don't kid yourself into thinking you're one of them.

Start to pay attention to what your ideal number of hours of sleep is per night. For me, eight is the magic number. If I get to sleep eight hours before I need to get up, I wake up naturally and feel my 100 per cent physical and mental best. If I get seven hours, I'm operating slightly substandard. Six hours, I'm fuzzy-headed, unfocused, lethargic and irritable.

Less than six hours – I'm a horrible bitch. The voice in my head becomes negative towards myself and others. I completely lack motivation. I feel emotional and sensitive, and I take it out on those I love the most.

If you're in the early days of motherhood or have a child who wakes in the night, you'll need to find ways to rest more, get some help and let go of thinking you can achieve all that you want to in a single day.

Then there's self-inflicted sleep deprivation – staying up too late even though you know you have to be up early. Many of the mothers I work with are now past the baby and toddler stage, yet they're getting to bed too late out of habit. They're depriving themselves of the deep benefits that come from getting enough sleep without fully realising the negative effects this has on their different life areas.

Arianna Huffington is so devoted to good sleep that she's written a whole book about it – *The Sleep Revolution: Transforming Your Life One Night at a Time*. I had the pleasure of meeting her and hearing her talk about the importance of sleep. Here were some of my biggest take-aways:

- Experiment with sleep times until you know how many hours of sleep you need.
- Determine what time you will need to turn the lights out based on what time you need to be up the next morning.
- Thirty minutes before lights-out, set an alarm as your 'shutting down time'. No computers, phones or TV allowed.
- Create a before-bed routine to wind down. Have a bath, climb into bed with a book. (Avoid anything too serious or disturbing.)

I now set an evening alarm to remind myself it's time to brush my teeth, wash my face and get into bed with an inspirational or personal growth book. I like to fill myself with a final dose of positivity before bed. If my husband is away I'll treat myself to a sleep meditation on the Insight Timer meditation app. My bed is my sanctuary and a place I absolutely love to crawl into.

The Power of
Your Breath

Most of us breathe too shallowly, hold our breath when we're stressed and don't get enough quality oxygen flowing through our body. It took professional breath coach Rebecca Dennis to truly wake me up to the immense power behind our breath. Rebecca's book *And Breathe* teaches simple ways to use conscious breathing for better health and wellbeing.

Breathing fully in and out releases tension, stress, anxieties, frustration and blockages that prevent us from living our best lives. I was so inspired after reading it that I booked in for a one-on-one session with Rebecca to learn about how to use Transformational Breath® to release old blockages and transform my energetic field. Wow – what an experience! Once I got the hang of the deep belly-breathing technique, I was able to access a higher state of consciousness and really hear my intuition. I received a lot of insightful advice from myself and I've acted on it with great results. I'm much more aware of my breathing in my everyday life and now catch myself holding my breath or breathing too much from my chest.

Maybe as you've been reading this you're already breathing more fully? This seems like a good time for a breathing pause . . .

Relax your shoulders and let out a deep sigh. Begin to notice the breath and become aware of the inhale and the exhale coming in and out like a wave. Breathe softly and deeply in through the nose and out through the nose with a little pause in between. As you inhale, guide the breath into the belly, encouraging a deep diaphragmatic breath.

Allow the mind to wander to the breath, and each time you notice you're going back into your thoughts, take your mind back to the breath.

Begin to draw your attention to the rise and fall of your breath.

Allow your breath to flow. No forcing it or pushing it. Gentle breathing. Expand your awareness inside and let go of the outside. There is nowhere to go, nothing to do. Just stay present with your breath.

Everything is as it should be right now. There is no wrong and there is no right. Stay present with your inhale and exhale.

Notice any thoughts that are there, not pushing them away, just taking the focus to the breath.

Deepen your breath connection by listening, observing the breath, and the thoughts should naturally become more distant and quieter.

Step outside the thoughts and observe them. Not entertaining them. Just allowing them to pass like clouds in the sky.

Breathe in and breathe out, letting go of anything that no longer serves you. Exhale away any tension worries. Inhale a new energy, positivity and light. Let go of the pull of the future and the pull of the past. Continue to go deeper inside. Explore and expand your awareness inside with each breath.

Stay in this moment, which is NOW. Keep practising this for two to three minutes and then notice how your mind feels.

—With thanks to Rebecca Dennis for this meditation.

Mindfulness and Meditation

Mindfulness is the practice of paying attention to your present-moment experience. When you're mindful, you observe your thoughts and feelings from a distance, without judging them good or bad. Practising mindfulness throughout your day is a way of returning your attention again and again to whatever you're doing or whom you're with. Your mind will naturally drift off into the future or past – or judge the situation you're in right now.

Mindfulness helps you turn down the volume on your busy brain. You begin to notice when you're off on a wild thought tangent and you're able to bring yourself back to the present moment – over and over, in a gentle way. The more you practise, the more easily you can handle strong emotions. It lowers your stress and anxiety levels, decreases the risk of depression and boosts your creativity.

A great tool to help you become more mindful is **meditation**. It gives you an opportunity to practise observing your thoughts with your eyes closed to the outside world as you focus on your breath.

It took me many years to finally get into a regular meditation practice. I was sure it would be good for me to quiet my mind and find peace within, yet all I seemed to accomplish in a session was mentally scanning my to-do list or pondering what I should make for dinner.

Finally I discovered guided meditations. They give my mind something positive to latch on to which slows down my busy brain. There are many meditation apps available, making it easy to listen to a guided meditation on your phone.

My absolute favourite is the free **Insight Timer Meditation** app with over 1,000 guided meditations to choose from. You can pick one based on how long you've got and within categories such as stress relief, relaxation, energy boosters, manifesting goals or to help you drift off to sleep – then bookmark your favourites to return to again. There's even one called 'A Breathing Space for Frazzled Moments' and plenty of choices for kids and teens so you can meditate together.

I can honestly say that my daily meditation habit has dramatically improved my life. I'm calmer and more patient, I worry less and let things go more easily, the voice in my head is nicer and my mind is no longer a runaway train. I've learned to gently observe my thoughts as they come and go, rather than get too attached to them. A few minutes meditating each morning make me more mindful the whole rest of the day.

YOU CANNOT
THINK A NEGATIVE
THOUGHT WHEN YOU

relax your forehead.

TRY IT RIGHT NOW

Depression

Most of us feel sad, down or gloomy from time to time. Feeling depressed can be a normal reaction to life's struggles: a loss, a knock-back, a rough patch that's taking a while to get through. SAD (seasonal affective disorder) strikes me when I don't get enough sunlight, but I now take vitamin D oil spray and St John's wort supplements in the winter months to keep it at bay. If you're experiencing feelings of intense sadness which last for weeks and keep you from functioning normally, your depression may be something deeper.

Everyone will have a different view of how to deal with depression. In her book *Happy*, Fearne Cotton, who has battled depression, says 'For me, medication was a last resort, and one I used only momentarily, but I'm thankful for the gear change the medicine provided so I could then look with clarity for other options for the long term.'

Fearne learned to recognise her ways of thinking that could lead her into feeling blue. She's aware of her triggers and can avoid certain situations or thought processes that could lead her down a dark and gloomy path.

There's nothing shameful about having a challenge that you can't solve on your own. Asking for help is a brave act and offering help to someone who may be depressed is tricky, but there are great resources out there to help. See the Health and Wellbeing resources (page 285) for more information.

Chronic Illness

A chronic illness is a condition that lasts for a very long time and usually cannot be cured completely, although some illnesses can be controlled or managed through lifestyle (diet and exercise) and certain medications. If you've been diagnosed with a chronic condition, it will be extra challenging to find a balance in life when your health requires so much attention.

> *Ever since I was diagnosed with Secondary Adrenal Insufficiency I have to closely guard my limited energy reserves and pick and choose carefully how I fill my day. If I overdo it, I can end up in a hospital bed attached to a drip. I've had to let go of the person I was before my illness was diagnosed. I spent a lot of time grieving for the woman I was – energetic, full of vitality and able to say yes to pretty much anything. I missed her so much and still do. After watching an amazing TED Talk by B. J. Miller titled 'What Really Matters at the End of Life' I totally reframed my thinking. I used my illness as an opportunity to redesign my life in the way I wanted to live it. I now know and respect the limits of my body, while embracing my soul and loving the person I am right here in this moment.*
>
> **—Anna**

If you've been diagnosed with a health issue or disease, you already know that other parts of your life are tipped out of balance with so much attention going on your health. Make adjustments in your expectations of what you can realistically achieve. What can you let go of? Where can you drop perfection or release guilt? Focus on what's good in your life to keep you vibrating on a positive frequency. Your body will thank you for it.

A little love note: *If the Health area of your life feels too difficult to start with right now, it could be that when you put your focus on another area, it may positively improve your health too. It's all interrelated. Be gentle with yourself and take things slow and easy.*

Take Action!

Use a Challenge Solver or an Ideas Into Action Sheet to get you moving on improving the Health area of your life. If time is your prevailing excuse, head to the Productivity chapter to find ways to make time for YOU and your health.

All Project Me Action Sheets can be found at www.myprojectme.com/action-sheets.

love

Love

Whether you're married, living with your partner, separated or divorced, if the Love area of your life is getting you down, this is your opportunity to dig deeper and ask yourself what's making you unhappy and what you can do about it.

The most important relationship you'll ever have is the one with yourself. We often think our partner needs to change in order for us to be happy. If only they'd stop doing this or start doing that. Your happiness cannot depend on another person changing. Our relationships are a mirror of the relationship we have with ourselves. The more you focus on the whole of your Project Me, the clearer this will become. Take the time to understand yourself and your relationship so you can make empowered choices that come from a place of confidence and inner wisdom.

In this chapter I will share some personal experiences about my own marriage, including what I do when this area of my life is challenging me. You'll find guidance for more serious struggles, such as drifting apart or deciding whether to stay or leave. I've called on some of my go-to experts on love, marriage, divorce and single motherhood for their words of wisdom to inspire you to take action. Take what you need, discard what you don't, but be proactive about your happiness.

Keeping the Connection

I consider myself to be very happily married but that's not to say we don't have to work on it. I constantly remind both of us that we are two separate people with two different upbringings, experiences and personalities, which means we simply aren't going to see eye-to-eye on everything. And we definitely don't! We made a pact when we decided to start a family that we would never become so child-centred that we'd put each other last.

Our kids are teenagers now and we're still going strong. I believe a lot of that has to do with making a real effort and not becoming complacent. Date nights sound so clichéd but I credit them with keeping our friendship strong. Going out without the kids and talking about stuff not related to home life is important to us and keeps us feeling fun, interesting and interested.

When we didn't have a babysitter, I'd organise a candlelit 'date' in our living room after the kids were tucked up in bed. I'd slip into something sexier than my sweatpants and we'd eat take-away sushi cross-legged at the coffee table, Japanese style. There were plenty of nights I'd planned a date, but was not in the mood when the time came. I kept my commitment to the plan and never regretted it.

Date nights are great, but everyday interactions are vital. We tell each other we love each other every day. And we hug, kiss, hold hands and send each other silly or sexy texts. We're completely honest with each other and we talk about any and everything.

I always thought maintaining connection would be easier once the kids were older and we were out of the trenches, but as they've grown into teenagers, a whole new challenge has presented itself. They stay up so late! Gone are the glory days of reading them a few bedtime stories, tucking them in and proceeding to have an evening to ourselves to eat a quiet dinner and cuddle up under a blanket watching a film or series. Now our kids are tucking us into bed! Or I can't fall asleep because I'm listening out for them to come home.

We have to adapt to the inevitable changes as our family life evolves. Once they leave home we'll have all the time in the world for each other. Which is why I'm glad we've put our marriage on the same level as our kids – giving equal importance to both.

> *For too long I'd been neglecting my relationship with my husband. The Life Wheel helped me recognise this and I've been working to correct it. We now have regular date nights (not necessarily out; it might be a nice home-cooked meal just for us). I also make sure we have a kiss and cuddle each day. Simple stuff that keeps us ticking over!*
>
> **–Elizabeth**

How to Treat Your Partner Like Your Best Friend

Imagine the scene: you've got a good friend visiting and she's brought some mud in on her shoes. Would you yell at her for not taking her shoes off? Demand she clean it up immediately? How about a friend drives you somewhere and takes a wrong turn. Would you make her feel like a dimwit? Cross your arms and get in a huff? And if she spilled some food down her front in a restaurant? Would you tut and shake your head in a 'can't take you anywhere' kind of way?

Of course you wouldn't! But what if the person in these scenarios was your partner? Hmm . . . The point is, we treat our friends more kindly than we do our own partner. Nit picking, nagging, snide comments – you'd *never* treat your close friends this way, yet it's easy to fall into this bad habit with a romantic partner.

I can't stand being treated like a child. I see red when my husband makes me feel worse for a mistake I'm already feeling bad about. Yet I know I'm guilty of criticising him in a way I'd never do with a girlfriend. When I remember to treat my husband more like a friend, guess what happens? He's nice back.

Four ways to give your partner the best friend treatment

1. Be interested.

Just as you'd listen attentively to a friend, do the same with your partner. Be aware of your body language, facial expression and tone. Stop what you're doing. Make eye contact. Be curious. Ask 'and then what happened?' – and genuinely mean it.

2. Show support.

If a friend shares a new goal or project she's excited about you'd share her enthusiasm, right? Instead of giving your partner a reality check on ten reasons why it'll never work, keep an open mind. If they are stressed about work, put yourself in their shoes and be supportive. You don't have to one-up them on what a bad day you've had.

3. Use the 5:1 rule.

Aim to say five kind things for every negative one. It can be hard to keep a daily track of this, but the gist is: say more nice things than bad.

4. Bite your tongue.

When you find yourself about to say something unkind or unhelpful – even if you're already mid-sentence – press your mental pause button. The more you practise, the better you get. Believe me! I was terrible at this before and I'm improving.

It's easy to get too comfortable and forget the basics of being kind and considerate. Give it a try and see what happens. They may just begin to give you the best friend treatment too.

Stuck in a Rut?
Drifting Apart?

Can you feel the distance between you growing? Is it difficult to remember a time when you felt genuinely connected? Maybe most of your conversations now revolve around the kids, the house and the grind of daily life and when it's just the two of you, you struggle with what else to talk about. You may have given up arranging date nights because it's too much hassle or expense to arrange babysitters – and what would you do anyway? Perhaps your social lives are becoming increasingly separate. In response you're relying more and more on your girlfriends for fun, adult conversation and connection. Or you're left on your own with the kids.

Awareness is the first important step in making any change in your life.

It's easy to become complacent – and boring – when you're busy raising young children. If you plan to be with your partner long after your kids have flown the coop, you mustn't wait until then to start having more fun together or you risk losing the very things that brought you together in the first place.

Start a 'Fun List' of things you can do together. Free things, paid things, stuff you used to do before kids, new ideas to try. Even holding hands on a walk together is a lovely way to build connection. Check local listings for live music, comedy, films, art, theatre, restaurants, bars, clubs. Join a gym or take a course together – like wine tasting, mindfulness or meditation. Take turns deciding what you'll do on a date night. Be open to each other's suggestions. Approach it with a fun and open attitude.

Check out the Fun and Friendships chapter and do the Fun Seeker Action Sheet on page 222 with your partner.

Is finding a babysitter an issue? Dig deep and ask yourself why. Is money too tight to ever go out, or could you find a way around it? Are you afraid to leave your child with someone else? It's normal to have anxieties in the beginning, but don't let that stop you from going out and enjoying some alone time with your partner. You brought this little person into the world because of your love for each other. Keeping your relationship fun and strong is a long-term gift for your child. A babysitter gets your child used to other authority figures and will greatly reduce their separation anxiety when they start school.

Katherine did her Life Wheel exercise and even though Love wasn't her lowest scoring life area, she decided that she valued her marriage too much to let it drop any lower than a five and wanted my help.

We do not make time for 'we' time – there is always something to do with the kids, house, tiredness, life . . . There's a lack of day-to-day intimacy and we have fun with friends, but rarely go out together. We've had these kinds of ups and downs before, but we haven't been this 'low' for a few years.

I got her to think about what a score of nine or ten would look like for her in her marriage. In her Dream Vision she described laughing more together, going out as a couple and having fun, as well as more playfulness and affection at home.

She made a Hot Power Statement:

I AM loving, sexy, exciting, attractive and confident. I create fun in our marriage. I choose this most important person to connect with every day.

I asked her to think about what could happen if she took no action and did nothing to improve the Love area of her life:

I could become bored and frustrated. I'd lose my fun and sexy side – shutting down that part of me. This could have consequences on everything else in my life – including my long-term happiness. We wouldn't grow old together and we'd miss out on so much!

Then she brainstormed some ideas for how to make her Dream Vision a reality. She created a small-step action plan that included:

- A twice-a-month date – taking turns with who chooses what to do and organising it.
- Sending playful texts.
- Initiating sex and day-to-day small acts of intimacy.
- Not keeping score on who has made the most effort. 'Just do more – don't keep score!' is her new mantra.

Three months later she wrote to say:

Our session totally turned things around. It was really powerful for me to visualise what a ten is for Love and I was so excited to start making it happen. The grandparents have taken the kids for a couple of nights and my husband and I are just about to go on a bike ride together!

Trouble Between the Sheets

Do you find yourself hoping your partner's already asleep when you crawl into bed? Finding it hard to muster up even a whiff of desire to make love? Worried your sex drive has dried up and disappeared forever? Not enough people open up about this problem, so that's what I want to do here.

Having a baby was all-consuming and my marriage went through a literal dry patch when my libido completely disappeared for many months. If my husband hadn't been so damn persistent about getting our sex life back on track, I'm not sure what would have happened.

I remember trying to act nonchalant at my local bookshop as the shopkeeper rang up my purchases: *The Seven Secrets of Mind-Blowing Sex* and *Mars and Venus in the Bedroom*, which I'd mixed in with *The Very Hungry Caterpillar* and *The Cat in the Hat*, only making it weirder.

Once a week we made a point of turning off the TV, lighting a few candles and trying to be romantic. Eventually my libido returned (hurrah!) and I was no longer going through the motions. We went through the whole thing again after our second child was born, but it was all worth it.

Maj Wismann, a leading Danish couples therapist and sexologist, assures new mothers that a lack of sex drive is completely normal and that nothing is wrong with you. She reminds us that being a new parent is a *huge* responsibility that comes with lots of worrying and adjustments. It's no longer just the two of you and it takes time to adapt to your new roles, new habits and new rhythms. All these adjustments require massive amounts of energy.

Maj says:

If you're breastfeeding you're producing the chemical called oxytocin, which is what helps strengthen the relationship between yourself and your baby. However, it does have the opposite effect on your sex drive hormones. The same goes for prolactin, another hormone you produce while breastfeeding. Prolactin is the chemical which is released after an orgasm and which makes you want to go straight to sleep. Sleep deprivation and exhaustion also play big roles in all of this. It's important to stop worrying about it and to shift your mindset into a proactive desire to slowly improve things.

Mismatched desires

If you're not a new mother, do know that it's normal for desire levels around sex to be mismatched in a relationship. Very often, one partner has a higher sex drive than the other. It's how you manage it that will make the difference to your relationship. **Communication is key.** You may be feeling stressed, anxious, hurt or annoyed. All of these things will affect your desire to be intimate with your partner. Let them know what's going on for you internally.

Isiah McKimmie is a couples therapist, sexologist and Tantra teacher who helps women and couples discover desire, sensuality and soulful intimacy. Isiah has some advice for any man or woman who feels guilty for turning down or avoiding sex:

When you turn down your partner's initiation of sex, they may feel rejected, unloved or fear that you're not attracted to them any more. These feelings can often lead to frustration and anger that really are just covering up their hurt and their longing to be connected with you. Build trust and love by telling them what you love and appreciate about them.

Maybe you don't want to 'give your partner the wrong idea' or 'lead them on' by being physically intimate with them when you're not in the mood for sex. Sadly, for many couples, this means that they're rarely physically intimate at all. Hugs and kisses dry up. You move away from their touch. You might not even be naked in front of them any more.

You might not feel in the mood for sex, but you can still stay connected and intimate through physical touch in a way that is nourishing for you.

Be clear with your partner that you don't feel like having sex, but tell them something that you would like to do with them. Could you cuddle? Swap a shoulder massage? Kiss?

Begin to work on your connection outside the bedroom too. Often a lack of desire shows up problems in the relationship as a whole. You might not spend as much time together or feel as close as you used to. Focus on your intimacy as a whole.

Above all, take care of yourself

You may feel just 'too tired' or like you don't have anything to give to your partner at the end of the day when you get into bed. Taking care of yourself will mean that you have more to give to your relationship and to your partner. When you feel nourished, alive and 'juicy', you bring that to your relationship and your relationship can feel nourished, alive and 'juicy' too.

Isiah says:

Take a look at your overall relationship and get help if you need to. Sometimes a lack of desire is symptomatic of other challenges going on in the relationship. You may need to take a step back and look at what else is going on between you and where the relationship is going. It can be challenging to break the cycles of your relationship and get things back. Professional help can make a real difference. You don't need to struggle with this alone.

Conflict Resolution

My hubby and I argue – loudly! Thanks to my Personal Growth efforts, it happens much less often these days. I recognise the role my ego plays in becoming defensive or wanting to win my point and I'm able to let go more easily when I've been triggered. Neither one of us is 'passive aggressive', which is sugar-coated hostility that builds up when you don't speak your mind or you're afraid to be honest and open. We're quite the opposite actually, saying whatever's on our mind – with volume and passion!

I used to worry about the kids hearing us argue, but I've come to realise that what's important is for them to see conflict resolution. One of us will hold out the olive branch – make a feeble apology or lightly touch the other to signify a desire to return to normal. The other will reluctantly accept. We do our best to stop things from escalating or dragging on as we find it emotionally exhausting to not get along.

The email trick

If you're having a real humdinger of an argument and neither one of you is backing down, try what we do and send an email. An email gives you a chance to articulate your feelings and put forward your side rationally. You can express yourself without being interrupted or defensive. Your partner can absorb what you're saying without added voice inflections, facial expressions or body language – and the kids won't hear you shouting.

Ideally your partner will read your words (without necessarily agreeing with them), feel touched by your desire to work things out – and respond in a like-minded way. Then, you'll have a chance to read their side and start making some serious progress towards reconciliation.

Recurring battles

If the same issues continuously reappear, put on your pro problem solver hat and see what you can do about it. Use a Challenge Solver Action Sheet (see page 34) to clearly define the issue on paper. Then brainstorm some ideas about how to solve it. Maybe you can do this together as a couple, but if not – don't let it stop you from doing it. Being the Project Manager of your life means taking charge of your happiness in your relationship.

EXPLAIN
YOUR
ANGER,
DON'T
EXPRESS IT,
AND THE
DOOR WILL
OPEN TO
SOLUTIONS
INSTEAD OF
ARGUMENTS.

Should I Stay or Should I Go?

'Wife Coach' Julie Marah works with women who are grappling with the decision of whether or not to stay in their relationship. She believes we need to do our own work first, getting to know and understand our own patterns of behaviour before we can figure out what we truly want to do. This allows us to make 'clean thinking' decisions. Once you stop pointing the finger of blame and take responsibility for your own happiness, you take back your power.

Relationships and marriages break down for all sorts of reasons. Many become dysfunctional and unhealthy. No woman ever leaves her marriage easily, or without a whole lot of soul-searching. There's a massive impact such a decision will have on our life and on those we love and care about the most. We don't take that decision lightly.

Julie encourages any woman to find a way to make her marriage work if that is what she truly wants. If the decision is made to leave, we don't have to blame and shame our husbands or partners, or ourselves. We don't have to feel guilty and selfish for prioritising our own happiness. We can give ourselves permission to create our lives in a way that allows us to live true to ourselves – without apology.

The impact of separation or divorce on your child

A huge fear in considering divorce is always the impact on your child. You want to do what's right for them. But kids will suffer more if you stay miserable in your marriage.

One mother said, 'My husband and I went through a trial separation and the number one fear was how it would affect our kids if we followed through with divorce. Living in separate households for three months changed the vibe that we had around each other. Our kids could feel this new loving energy. At first the energy wasn't toward each other; it was an inner peace and calm that we had stopped fighting.'

Certified divorce coach Summer Howard shares her own personal story:

I wanted so much for my child's life to be happy, supported and free from pain. But, the reality was that she witnessed a relationship steeped in resentment and functioning out of a complete communication breakdown. I experienced a deep knowing that if my kiddo could grow up with two happy parents instead of two miserable parents, then she would have a better chance for a healthy self-esteem and make better choices when choosing her life partner.

Although I think both my husband and I felt like there was too much 'water under the bridge' of our relationship . . . it was clear that the change had to happen with me.

So I did it.

My unending love for my child was the reason I chose to leave and the reason I chose a happier life. At the time, as crushing as it was to lose my partner and my dreams for a healthy marriage, after I got over the initial shock, I felt free. As if I'd been lifted out of an oppressive situation.

Five years after my decision to leave, our child is happily living in two loving homes with blended families and she has more love in her life than seems humanly possible.

I was clear about my decision, and even though it hurt like hell at first, I am so very glad I had the clarity and vision to see a better life for all of us.

If you are concerned about the impact divorce will have on your child, please take a deep, long breath. Exhale and know this to be true:

My child will be OK because I am doing the best that I can.
I love my child and I show them how I love them through my words and my actions.
I listen to my child's concerns and their hurts.
I know that through the easy and the hard times they can rely on me to be a rock and to show them how to make decisions with a sure, confident and loving heart.
I believe life will truly be better for us all.

— Summer Howard
Bridge to Bliss

Life During Divorce

Whether it was your decision or not – the decision to divorce is a bitter pill to swallow. You might feel that you have failed, that everyone will be judging you for not holding on to your marriage. The truth is, nobody on the outside can ever know what goes on between a couple behind closed doors.

Vivienne Smith of *The Single Mum's Survival Guide* provides support, practical advice and inspiration to single mothers. She says:

> You don't need to talk about all the gory details if you don't want to. You can justifiably answer prying questions by repeating 'I'd rather not talk about it'. If you do want to confide in somebody (and I believe we all need help and encouragement and that's how we women get through things), then make sure you pick someone who will make you feel safe and supported. The best help they can give you is to be a sympathetic sounding board and allow you to reach your own conclusions.
>
> Even if your split is amicable, divorcing with the minimum of damage to yourselves and any children you might have together requires thought and preparation and a large dose of courage and honesty. These days the legal system has undergone many changes to encourage a less combative approach and this is a very positive development, but the reality of your situation will be dictated by how you and your ex approach proceedings and each other. There will be no winners from a bitter, protracted divorce and your pockets will be a lot lighter. Choose legal representation as soon as possible. Don't be afraid to shop around to find a lawyer that you feel comfortable with – most will offer an initial no-cost consultation before you sign on the dotted line.
>
> Do-it-yourself divorces are risky and a false economy that may come

back to bite you later on down the line. However, you can avoid huge legal bills by doing some preparation and having a clear plan. Avoid mudslinging and strive to remain as dignified as possible with your ex during the process. Do not use your lawyer as an emotional coach or sounding board. They are doubtless sympathetic to your plight but their job is to advise you legally; use a trained coach or therapist to work through the inevitable emotional rollercoaster that you will be experiencing. Agreement is far more quickly reached if you show a reasonable attitude and you are realistic about what you hope the outcome will be.

Please remember that however dark and depressing divorce may seem, you will walk in the sunlight again. Be on the lookout for unexpected gifts and happiness – perhaps a feeling of freedom and possibility, the sense that now you have a choice and it's up to you to design the life you truly deserve. Celebrate small victories in any way you see fit. Allow some time alone to process and grieve the death of your relationship but at the same time don't withdraw from the world – go out there and get stuck into life once more. It's time to rejoin the land of the living and start on your new path. One day you might look back with the perspective that can only be gained by distance and realise that this crisis was the catalyst for something incredible and so much better for your health and happiness than you could ever have imagined in that dreary and dismal time.

Life After Divorce

Will I ever love again? Can I ever be loved again? You may be asking yourself these questions. Please know – you are not ruined by divorce. **You are worth being loved.** Start by learning to love yourself.

Love yourself by taking care of yourself. Get good sleep, eat well, get fresh air and exercise, fill yourself with positive inspiration and surround yourself with those who lift you higher. Focus on your Project Me. Be proactive about bringing a greater sense of balance into your life.

Forgive yourself for a failed marriage. When you forgive, you also show others how it's done. Find a way to let go of grudges. When you catch yourself thinking painful or vengeful thoughts about your ex, take a deep breath and let it go. In the beginning you may be doing this over and over and over again. With time, as you keep experiencing the brief relief of letting go, you will one day find that you truly have. Forgiveness heals. It makes us more positive. It increases our ability to help others. It increases our ability to help ourselves.

When you love yourself, let go of the past and focus on the now: you are changing your vibrational frequency and without much effort you will attract love into your life. Believe this to be true.

the most important relationship I have is with

myself

#ProjectMe

Finding Love Again

Ready to dip your toe back in the water? Wondering what the rules are for dating again? Vivienne Smith says:

In my experience, internet dating is still the easiest way to find prospective partners. It's been fun, fascinating, sometimes sad and on occasion downright hilarious! I discovered that looking through people's profiles was a little like looking through a catalogue. It's certainly heartening to see just how many fish there are in the sea . . .

Make the first date casual – a coffee or a walk and drink. Don't put too much pressure on the occasion. Remember that your first meeting is really a way to see if there might be something worth exploring in more detail on subsequent meetings. If you do decide to take it further, make sure that you are moving at a rate that you are comfortable with. If you ever feel pressured or panicky, listen to your intuition and extricate yourself as quickly as possible. Be mindful of your own emotional wellbeing and aware that you may be at your most vulnerable right now. If it feels too soon to be looking for a relationship then just close the door for the time being. You can always revisit this place when you are feeling stronger and more confident.

Make sure that you only introduce your new partner to your children when you are reasonably confident that this will be a long-term relationship. It can be confusing for children to meet too many 'friends' and it also puts the pressure on your new relationship. Take time to enjoy each other and get to know each other properly before introducing anybody else into the mix. Ask yourself: am I feeling happy? Do I feel respected? Can I be myself? Do I have peace of mind with this person? If yes, then go ahead and have some fun. You deserve it and as long as you stay safe and it's not affecting anyone else, then why not? But give it time. If it's right then you can take it slow and enjoy each other. There's no need to rush to the next stage just now. If it's right then you can enjoy the journey. What's the hurry? On the other hand, they may really be the best thing that could ever happen, so don't be so suspicious or wary that you let true love slip through your fingers.

Take Action!

Don't just read about it, do something about it. If any ideas have been sparked as you've read this chapter, use an Ideas Into Action Sheet to come up with three small steps you can take straight away.

Use a Challenge Solver Action Sheet if you're feeling stuck about where to begin. Be sure to check out the Love resources at the end of this book for lots of extra support.

All Project Me Action Sheets can be found at www.myprojectme.com/action-sheets.

work

Work

It's been said that there are three types of women:

1. The women who chose career and feel conflicted by that choice.
2. The women who chose family and feel conflicted by that choice.
3. The women who chose family and career and feel conflicted by that choice.

If you're here because you're feeling conflicted about the Work area of your life, you're definitely not alone.

Juggling work and family life isn't easy. Whether you work full-time or part-time, at home or away, it leaves you with less to give the other seven areas of your life. It's an ongoing challenge to try to squeeze it all in.

Equally, if you've given up work to raise kids, you may have a nagging feeling that you 'should' be working, or perhaps you need to return to work for financial reasons. Maybe you've lost your confidence or you worry that you won't find work that fits in around family.

Open your mind to the possibility of being a fourth type of woman:

The woman who chose family and career and feels fulfilled by that choice.

For some women this happens naturally (and those women are probably not heading to this chapter of the book anytime soon!), and for others (like me), it's a journey.

Since becoming a mother I've worked, not worked, worked freelance, done volunteer work, and eventually set up an online business of my own. And, of course, I've written this book along the way!

I've been fortunate enough to not have to work, as my husband works his tail off to be our main breadwinner. I'm motivated to turn my online business into one that enables him to step away from the daily nine to five (in reality more like seven to seven) and finally relax more and enjoy life.

I've witnessed first-hand how hard women can be on each other for the career choices they make. Loitering on both sides of the playground fence means that I've heard the non-working mothers judge the ones that work and vice versa.

There is no right or wrong and it's time to drop the judgement, guilt and self-doubt.

If the Work area of your life is getting you down, it's time to figure things out. The next section is divided into some potential scenarios you might relate to. See if any of them resonate and spark some ideas, then write them down and brainstorm. This sets the wheels in motion and things begin to fall into place naturally. You'll suddenly hear of opportunities that would have washed right over you before.

My Treasure Trove of Resources at the end of this book are gold and will help you get further clarity over your career options (see page 288).

Maternity Leave

Should I stay or should I go? My story

BC (Before Children), I had a fun and exciting job in the entertainment industry. Parties, concerts and gigs were all part of the package and my self-image was very intertwined with my career.

When I became pregnant I had to decide whether to take the maternity package on offer or cut the cord (so to speak) and be a SAHM (stay-at-home mum).

My head was in a total spin over it.

Then I got proactive. I did what I do best and got it out of my head and onto paper with a good old-fashioned pros and cons list. Next, I used another potent tool: visualisation. I closed my eyes and imagined what my daily life would look like in each scenario.

My visualisation looked like this:

Option A: Take maternity leave and return to work.
- Find someone I trust implicitly to look after my baby for nine hours a day, five days a week. Get dressed and ready on little sleep, hand baby over and commute into the office.
- Work all day, commute home, and have baby again at the 'arsenic hour' when everyone's tired and cranky.

Option B: Quit my job and stay at home.
- Be at home with my baby 24/7.
- No creative outlet or non-baby-related interaction with adults; potential to be bored senseless.

- Earn no income.
- Lose an essential part of my identity.

Writing it all down like this made me realise that I wanted the best of both worlds. To keep my creative cogs turning, continue earning money, still feel like 'me' – but to also be a big part of my baby's daily development and not feel completely dependent on someone else to look after him. I already loathed my daily commute and wanted to drop that from my life.

Then the solution came to me.

I'd work from home as a freelance graphic designer, hire a part-time nanny and take on only as much work as I could calmly handle.

I promptly handed in my notice and used the remainder of my pregnancy to set up my home business. I already had the graphic design skills; now I needed to make it work for me in a whole new setting.

For a while it was a successful solution. I organised things like baby swimming lessons and musical playgroups on the days we had together and hired an amazing nanny to help on the days I worked. I never felt I missed anything as they were only downstairs and I could pop in and say hello anytime.

You can only guess which days I found more utterly exhausting and challenging! On the mornings when our nanny arrived, I felt an enormous surge of gratitude as she walked in the door. But I also cherished my days with my son and appreciated the balance of both realities.

However, my happy little set-up took on some fresh challenges when baby number two came along. I share that story over in the Family chapter but, in a nutshell, I morphed into a super-stressed mama until I finally did some parenting skills classes and then went on to create my Project Me.

Every situation is different and you need to weigh your own set of pros and cons

There's no point judging anyone else's choices. What's right for your best friend isn't necessarily right for you. But it's important that the career choice you make is done consciously and with an understanding of the options open to you.

Many mothers feel trapped in an old unsuitable career after having children. Others leave work, then feel they're not using their brains or are wasting years of education and training. Both don't realise that their skills, experience and gifts could be shared with the world in a different way.

If you're considering a return to work, it's important to honestly assess your situation and understand your true motivations. Whether you're returning to work because of finances, because you want adult interactions, or because you enjoy your career, get clear about why you want it and what the benefits will be to you and your family. Be confident in your decision. If you've weighed it all up and you're leaning in favour of staying home, be just as confident with that choice. Nothing's carved in stone and you're allowed to change your mind later if something interesting presents itself or your circumstances change.

A Smooth Return to Work

If you've made the decision to take maternity leave and return to work, you'll make a smoother transition if you get the Productivity area of your life into a good place. Consider practicalities, such as childcare arrangements, meal planning, food shopping and housework, as well as self-care. Establish sustainable working hours so you can find a balance that feels right for you. Have a think too about ways to build a strong support network, whether that be paid back-up help or friends and family.

The more confident you are, the more ready you'll be to handle fresh challenges at work and at home. Career confidence coach Sherry Bevan encourages women to find a coach or other supporters who'll be cheerleaders on your side, bolstering your confidence on days you feel down. Having an accountability partner will keep you on track with your goals and intentions. Read about how to create a Power Posse in the Fun and Friendships chapter (page 217). You may need two or three people to give you the emotional support you need.

Mama Guilt

One demon you'll need to face is the guilt that comes with work. Or the guilt that comes with not working! Thoughts like:

I shouldn't be working – my kids need more attention.
I should be working so we can afford more for the kids/I can be a better role model for my
daughter/I can use my brain.
I didn't spend enough time playing with my child today.
I didn't get anything done today because I was playing with my child.
I let my kids eat too much junk/play too many computer games.
I'm too strict/too lenient/too inconsistent.

The list goes on and on and on . . .

Look at the part perfectionism may be playing in your guilt. Are you being too hard on yourself? Trying to be everything to everyone? Taking on too much and then feeling guilty when you can't manage to do everything? Perhaps you have unrealistic expectations about what you can achieve in the hours available?

Some guilt can serve a useful purpose by acting as a signal for when you're not living in alignment with your values. Those uncomfortable pangs may help you to pay closer attention and motivate you to do things differently.

Take Action!

When you notice yourself repeatedly feeling waves of guilt over something, hash it out on paper with a Challenge Solver Action Sheet (page 34). Be honest about whatever's making you feel like a 'not good enough' mother/wife/daughter/friend and once you've identified the triggers, brainstorm some ideas for what to do about it.

What about all of those things you feel guilty about that you can't really change? Too often it's our perception that we're hurting someone or doing something that we believe to be wrong.

Sherry Bevan says:

> Guilt is a complex emotion. What is important is that you acknowledge and investigate the guilt that you feel. Then you can decide whether or not that guilt is justified and whether you want to do something about it. It's important to appreciate yourself and what you do as a mother. Take stock of your current situation, your strengths, your experiences and your skills. These are different for every woman, for every mother, for every parent.

Remind your mean inner critic that you're doing the best you can with what you've got. You're in control of your own happiness and persistent guilt will only zap your energy and wear you down. Show yourself the compassion and love that you deserve and stop beating yourself up. You're doing much better than you think.

Journal Prompt

★ What is special about me as a mother?

★ What do I do for my child that nobody else does?

★ What are my limitations?

★ What are my boundaries?

★ What stops me doing more or less or different?

★ What are my strengths?

★ What are my special skills?

MAMA MANTRA

FEELING GUILTY DOES NOT MAKE ME GUILTY.

#PROJECTME

Being a SAHM

Some stay-at-home mothers wouldn't trade it for the world; others feel unfulfilled and frustrated in this role. Most vacillate between loving it and going nuts several times during the course of one day! Being at home with the kids is a rollercoaster ride of highs and lows.

If you find yourself in a complaining trap, take a moment to figure out what's making you unhappy so you can do something about it.

Start by identifying the problem.

- Lacking Me Time?
- Feeling overwhelmed?
- Need extra help?
- Bored and uninspired?
- Uncooperative child?
- Unsupportive partner?

Once you've zeroed in on what the main issues are, brainstorm some potential options. Break those down into three simple small-step actions you can take.

For example, if you've identified that your biggest frustration is feeling lonely and bored at home with your young child, what small things could you do to breathe some fresh air into your daily life? Could you join a mother and toddler group? Find a local gym with a crèche? Explore one of the many online mama friendship matching services that are springing up? See the Fun and Friendships chapter for inspiration.

Getting the help you need

Many SAHMs feel that because they're at home, they shouldn't need to enlist the help of others, paid or otherwise. But doing it all on your own is incredibly exhausting. Happy mothers ignore the guilt and get help as they see fit. Being able to food shop solo or head out for a run or a much-needed girlie lunch does wonders for a mama's soul.

Maybe you want to outsource some of the cleaning or laundry so you can be more present with your child. Perhaps some kiddie-free time is what you need. Go get some exercise, run errands or get your hair done. You're a better mother when you're not overwhelmed and stressed, so don't be afraid to explore options for getting the help that will make you happier.

It's also important to accept help when it's offered. Seriously. Anytime anyone offers to help, take them up on it. The quicker you come around to this idea, the easier your life's going to get. People like to help. It releases feel-good endorphins. You'll have plenty of opportunities to reciprocate, so grab those precious offers.

Asking for help can feel trickier, but you'll get the hang of it. It's all about *how* you ask. I always preface my request with, 'I've got a favour to ask and it's absolutely OK if you can't do it because I can ask someone else – no problem.' And I genuinely mean it. I'm good at reading someone whose mouth is agreeing to help but whose face is showing inconvenience, and I won't let them accept. I have a strong enough support network to call on someone else. My friends know that if it's no extra hassle for me, I'll readily help them with school runs, collecting from parties or having their child over for a play date or sleepover.

Consider who might be able to help:

- Your partner/kids
- Parents/in-laws/other relatives
- Older siblings
- Friends
- Neighbours
- Paid help

See the Productivity chapter for tips on assembling your support squad (page 63).

I

A S K

FOR HELP.

I

DROP

PERFECTION.

#PROJECTME #MAMAMANTRA

Embrace the chaos

As much as I'm a fan of enlisting extra help, there's also a lot to be said for embracing chaos. This is something I wish I'd done more of when my kids were little. The house doesn't need to be spotless, dinner doesn't need to come from a celebrity cookbook and routines can be loosened on occasion. You don't have to be the perfect mother. It's good to let yourself off the hook a lot more often and stop beating yourself up. Don't take things so seriously.

Finding Work that Fits in Around Family

I hear from many mothers who've been out of the workforce since starting a family and now feel confused and apprehensive about if or when they want to jump back in.

Many make the choice to be a SAHM when the kids are little, but later wish they hadn't let their skills and contacts lapse to the point where they've lost confidence in their abilities. Others aren't excited about returning to work but need or want to contribute to the family income or would like some financial independence.

A big concern is finding work that fits in with family life. Unlike mothers who returned to work straight after maternity leave, women who've had years at home with the kids can't imagine not dropping them off/picking them up from school, or not being at all of their events. They worry about what would happen if their child were at home sick or what they'd do about childcare during school holidays.

I put this topic out to the members of my Project Me Goal Diggers group to hear what they had to say about finding work that fits in with family. It got a very strong reaction, mostly from those who are feeling perplexed about what to do next.

I'm completely petrified at the thought of going back into the workplace after ten years' break! I'm really interested in finding out what I really want to do workwise that's meaningful and worthwhile and how that would fit in with family life.

—Louise

I made the choice when my kids were little to be a stay-at-home mother. Now my kids are teenagers I feel like I 'should' be back at work. I would love to be contributing some money but I don't want to be back working corporate hours, or have work stress – running the family is enough! I feel like I need to be a better role model for my daughter who recently commented about me 'having nothing to do all day'. I'm concerned about not fitting in anywhere any more, what I would actually like to do and how I could use my skills.

—Jan

I was out of the workplace for over seven years and there had been immense changes in the industry, as you can imagine, but after two and a half years back in the saddle I'm more senior than I was pre-kids and so much wiser. It's hard but not impossible. Earning my own money is liberating and gives me choices.

—Kathryn

I only had a one-year break with both kids, but I remember that when it was time to go back I was scared of no longer being able to do my job and use my brain. Also I was dreading the amount of work in the office and at home (and I'm still overwhelmed). But I'm so happy I'm working, no matter how difficult it is to organise everything.

—Paola

Miisa Mink is the founder of DrivenWoman, a women's LifeWorking™ network where like-minded women support each other to achieve their goals. Here's her advice for mothers who are struggling to know where to begin when it comes to finding work that fits around family:

- Tell others that you're looking to find work. Research shows that people who share their goals are much more likely to achieve them.
- Talk to people beyond your usual set of friends. You have to step outside your comfort zone to get inspired by new stories.
- Join or form a group of like-minded women so you can all support each other. Once you start speaking about wanting to find work you love, you're opening yourself up to ideas and opportunities.
- Seek out mentors – people who are already living a lifestyle you want. Find out how they have got to where they are and see which parts of their journey you can emulate.
- Start a fresh notebook for brainstorming ideas and collecting research. The ideas will start to flow once you do this, so don't wait.

Flexible Working Hours

Flexible working is a way of working that suits the employee's needs, such as having flexible start or end times or working from home. It can also mean working part-time, reduced hours or jobsharing. If you plan to work for a company outside the home, consider what kind of schedule would suit you and request flexible working.

Alex Brown is the creator of The Joy Of Flex, championing flexible working hours to keep talented women in the workforce. She shares her advice for anyone seeking a more flexible working arrangement with their employer:

> Suggest a trial run. Flexibility relies on trust and respect from both sides and an ongoing dialogue about what's working and what can be improved, which in turn helps to build a strong working relationship.
>
> When formally asking to change a full-time role into a flexible role, make a solid case for why you should work flexibly. Focus on what the business will be getting out of the arrangement, not just why it would suit you. Plan the conversation and anticipate all potential push backs; think about a solution to every possible issue. There are lots of online resources that can help you plan your conversation. It's worth reading up on workplace rights and negotiation techniques as being well prepared will help you feel more confident. Your employer will get more from you in a flexible arrangement than less, so put yourself first and go for it. What have you got to lose?
>
> Don't be afraid to look elsewhere if the company you work for doesn't support you. Push out of your comfort zone and into the job market. You never know what amazing opportunity is around the corner.

Head to the Work resources (page 288) to find websites that'll support your search, then make a plan. Break it down into tiny doable steps. Small steps will get you there!

I AM ABUNDANTLY SUCCESSFUL IN EVERYTHING I DEDICATE MYSELF TO

#PROJECTME

Starting Your Own Business

If you're considering setting up your own business, you'll probably have a lot of fears and doubts about whether your idea is going to work or not. Who will buy from you? How will you find customers or clients? How will you set your prices? Where do you even begin?

Whether you want to set up a local business or if you're more drawn to the online world, working for yourself can be incredibly rewarding and challenging in equal measure.

People often ask what it's like to be an online entrepreneur at myprojectme.com. The truth is, it's the most creative and fulfilling work I've ever done. Starting something completely from scratch and building it into a successful business makes me feel very proud. I've learned how to do countless new things, from setting up a website to creating and growing a newsletter mailing list, to making videos and managing social media platforms.

By far, the most rewarding part of it all is helping others. If you can find work you love that serves others, you're onto something particularly magical. They say the most successful businesses are the ones that solve a problem and Project Me is all about teaching problem-solving skills to busy mothers.

It was the summer of 2012 when I read a book called *The Millionaire Messenger: Make a Difference and a Fortune Sharing Your Advice*. With wide-eyed wonder I devoured Brendon Burchard's words about how to make a difference to the world by packaging your knowledge and advice on any topic to help others succeed. I wrote down the answers to these questions:

What do you know more about than someone else?

I was a mother of a teen and a tween, so I guess I knew more about motherhood than a new mother . . . And I suppose I knew more about parenting skills, time management and personal growth than someone who'd never read half of the books I've consumed on those subjects.

What's a topic you've always been passionate about or a topic you'd like to help other people to master?

Journaling and problem solving on paper. Having clear, written goals and dreaming BIG.

What have you overcome and how?

I'd definitely overcome a lot of my parenting challenges by then. I'd given up the screaming and now had a harmonious family life. I'd also learned how to find a happier balance across my different life areas and had a lot of tools and strategies under my belt.

What's something I do anyway without even being paid? What do others compliment me on for being good at?

I was always hooking friends up with resources that were helping me and they always thanked me for that. People often remarked that they felt very inspired and motivated after speaking to me. I realised I had a way of giving people advice that didn't seem pushy or know-it-all.

Asking myself these questions made me see that I had a potentially marketable talent I could combine with my graphic design background.

Consider what you have to offer. You probably have more knowledge or experience in an area than someone else. You don't have to be a world-renowned expert on it and it doesn't matter if others are already offering their insights on it. You are you – with your own unique voice and angle on it. Identify an audience that would be served by your experience and knowledge, figure out what they're struggling with the most and come up with ideas on how you can help them.

I know I'm making that sound very simplistic, but in many ways it is. It's what you do with it from there that takes further figuring out.

Use your journal to explore your own answers to the four questions above and see if this sparks any potential business ideas.

Online business school

I was fortunate enough to stumble across Marie Forleo, who quickly became my online business guru as she knew everything I didn't know about how to build an online presence and attract my ideal customers to my website. A website that didn't exist yet!

Marie runs a six-week online business training programme called B-School once a year, and I grabbed a spot in the programme the day before the deadline to enrol. I honestly don't know how I'd have done it without Marie's B-School, particularly her online forum of fellow female entrepreneurs, all sharing what we knew and supporting one another.

At this point my fabulous friend Suzie was on board and together we learned the ins and outs of it all. Having a business partner kept me accountable and motivated, even during the technically challenging times. At that point, even setting up domain names and company email addresses was time-consuming and exhausting. We shared the blogging and editing load, attempted to learn about SEO (search engine optimisation) and compiled mountains of research into the 8 Key Life Areas for Project Me.

I happily worked on Project Me while my two kids were in school, but Suzie had to juggle it with her yoga teaching schedule and raising four children. It wasn't long before the balanced life we were promoting wasn't ringing true for her. Something had to give and reluctantly, with great sadness on both of our parts, Suzie decided to step away from Project Me to devote more time to her family and yoga business. I didn't blame her. The business was making no money after its outgoing running costs.

Inspiration and Passion

I was nowhere near throwing in the towel and flying solo gave me focus and determination. I decided to create an online goal-setting programme, which was an immediate success. I loved working with mothers from all over the world, understanding the common struggles we share and offering my tools and support. From there I did one-on-one Skype sessions, eventually giving productivity coaching to a mother who happened to be a top literary agent. She went on to represent me for this very book you're reading right now.

I share this to inspire you to find something you're passionate about and see where that takes you. Maybe now, maybe in a few years' time, but don't wait for everything to be perfect before you begin brainstorming your ideas on paper. All it takes is the seed of an idea and the curiosity to see where it may lead.

Whether your business idea is product or service based, local or online, you'll need to carve out plenty of time and be self-motivated enough to keep going even when the going gets tough. The more balanced your life is before you embark on a new business venture, the easier you'll find it.

I MAKE
MY IDEAS

HAPPEN

Volunteer Work

If you're in a position where you don't need or want to work, consider doing some rewarding volunteer work. You could find a one-off opportunity such as a charity event or something more long-term on a set day each week. There are also plenty of flexible volunteering posts for offering your services as and when it suits you. Volunteering helps you to learn new skills to increase future employability, plus the added benefits of getting out there, meeting interesting people and making a difference.

I'd always longed to do some kind of volunteer work, but never made it happen until our family moved to Madrid for my husband's job. Instead of diving back into my freelance graphic design work, I decided to spend some time immersing myself in Spanish culture and learning the language.

I volunteered at a local soup kitchen every Monday. There's nothing like mingling with the locals to improve your vocabulary! The older Spanish ladies kindly put up with my poor grammar and patiently slowed down their chatter so I could stand a chance of following their gossip and hilarious stories. On school holidays I'd take my kids along with me. The ladies immediately put them to work unpacking boxes and sorting fruits and vegetables.

Finding a volunteer job that suits your personality and schedule is now easier than ever thanks to websites that list opportunities in your area. Volunteering at your child's school is another way to get involved, meet other parents and get to know the behind-the-scenes stuff a lot better. I reluctantly put my hand up to be class rep for my son's year group and it turned out to be a wonderful experience for both of us.

Take Action!

If you'd like to move yourself into a higher score in the Work area on your Life Wheel, this is your opportunity. The best ideas flow when you put pen to paper with a Challenge Solver or Ideas Into Action Sheet. For more inspiration and support, explore my Treasure Trove of Resources at the back of this book.

All Project Me Action Sheets can be found at www.myprojectme.com/action-sheets.

fun

Fun and Friendships

In the wake of everything else that needs doing, it's easy to forget about having fun. And when the fun dries up, so do you. Maybe you're feeling stuck in a rut and your fun-o-meter is registering 'bored'. It could be that you're having some friendship issues or that you're simply not seeing enough of your friends.

We all have our own definition of what's fun. And that definition changes at different stages of your life. Rather than comparing the Fun area of your life to what it was BC (Before Children), redefine what fun means to you at the stage you're at right now.

Imagine that your life story is made into a book. It begins with your childhood, followed by early adulthood. Then starts your motherhood chapter – all about raising your family. The entire second half of the book centres on your life *after* your child or children have flown the coop.

Now imagine that each chapter has its own subheadings. If you're in the big, juicy parenting chapter, which subheading are you currently in? Deep in the baby/toddler trenches? Primary school with a bit more flexibility? The teenage years?

This parenting-kids-who-still-live-at-home period may feel long now, but in the bigger scheme of things, it's but one chapter of your life. **Always remember: you have much more of your life to live after your kids become adults.** This doesn't mean waiting until then to start having fun again – on the contrary. The more fun you weave into your life now, the easier it's going to be to continue to have fun later on. Fun is a mindset. Keeping a sense of light-heartedness and fun is a quality that'll always serve you well.

Even if you don't have a lot of spare time or energy to go out looking for fun, don't resign yourself to thinking that your fun days are behind you. If you have an absolute laugh playing with your child, do count that time towards the Fun area of your life. All laughter is good laughter! But if you're in need of some kiddie-free fun, don't feel guilty about it.

Want some ideas to up your Fun score? You're in the right place.

Take Fun Seriously

Always begin with knowing what you want. What would a nine or a ten look like in this life area for you? Get that vision clear in your mind, as well as why you want to have more fun and what would happen if you did nothing to improve this area. This alone will get you thinking and will lead to some initial ideas to get things flowing.

Adela chose to focus on the Fun area of her life. She said:

Choosing to focus on fun seemed at first like too much ME ME and rather frivolous. Then I realised I've been putting so much effort into the other areas for so long and feel I have lost sight of this part and lost the FUN! I've reached a point where I need to reconnect with me. I want to feel that I have more time for positive things to feed my soul and find ways and time to do some things I love – and to even remember and discover what they are. This feels like a good place to start and of course I deserve some fun!

I encouraged Adela to visualise what the Fun area of her life would look and feel like if she'd given it a higher score. She wrote her Dream Vision and from that she created a Hot Power Statement:

I AM a fun person, connected to my husband and family and an expanded group of friends through shared interests. I feel part of a community. I enjoy experiencing cultural activities both with others and on my own and have a social network which includes some strong friendships. I FEEL connected, engaged and enriched.

She then used an Ideas Into Action Sheet to brainstorm some ways to make her Dream Vision her reality. A few weeks later, here's what Adela said:

I think choosing fun was hard – partly because it is so linked to how we feel about ourselves. It is hard to go out and be a fun friend if you're feeling overloaded with other things in your life. However, it was good to think about what fun elements I lacked and what I needed to feel a bit more like ME. I started saying YES to more things and via a Facebook connection I ended up going to the cinema during the day with a mum from school. I wouldn't have allowed myself to do that if I'd not been thinking about taking fun seriously. I've also started doing a jewellery-making class and I no longer beat myself up for taking time out to do coffee or lunches with friends rather than always just getting things done. Since Project Me I've become more rooted locally in my community and there's definitely more fun in my life.

Elaine is another mother who decided to focus on Fun. She had no idea what she was about to unleash once she put her mind to it!

Life was so full-on that I'd forgotten to stop, look around and get clear on my priorities. As I entered my fiftieth year and started working on my Project Me, I began doing things that previously I would have written off as not possible. I did the Rickshaw Run in India, travelling 4,500km in a tuk-tuk for charity, which was incredibly fun. I then cycled through Namibia! I honestly didn't think I had it in me, but because I stopped procrastinating and started to set some juicy goals to have fun, I pushed the boundaries of what I thought was possible.

Fun Seeker Action Sheet

It's time to get your cogs turning about how to inject more fun into your life.

Use the **Fun Seeker** Action Sheet to explore what fun means to you. Add any ideas that come to you as you read this chapter. Some of these can happen now; others may have to simmer gently on the back burner until you have more time, freedom or money. It's fun in itself to get juiced up about future fun and begin any preliminary research or planning.

If you think of any friends or family members you'd like to join you, jot their names next to your ideas.

You may draw a blank on some of the questions at first. Don't judge yourself for this. Leave it for now and you may find that over the next few days and weeks more ideas will flow once you've opened up the channels.

A printable copy of the Fun Seeker Action Sheet is yours for the taking at www.myprojectme.com/action-sheets.

Project Me

☺ Fun Seeker ☺

What did I used to find fun, but haven't done lately?

What have I been meaning to try, but haven't yet?

What would I do if time and money were no object?

Is there a smaller, doable version of the above I could do now?

Which hobbies would I love to resume / do more often / start new?

If I could take a class (online or in person), what would I like to learn more about or learn how to do?

Which concerts / plays / exhibitions would I love to see?	Which publications / websites show local listings of events and things to do in my area?
Who could I invite for coffee / lunch / dinner?	What kind of volunteering / charity event could I get involved in?

Now circle any ideas above you particularly like. **Take control of your own FUN and start taking ACTION!**

WWW.MYPROJECTME.COM

Explore Your Personality

Part of becoming the expert of you in the Fun and Friendships area of your life is exploring your own personality and understanding where you are on the introvert–extrovert spectrum.

It's taken me years to understand my own introverted tendencies. I think of myself as a very social person, yet there are times when I feel quite the opposite. As I approach the school gates to collect my kids, I see mothers all talking in small groups. My chest clenches up as I scan the crowd, trying to look nonchalant or busying myself on my phone. Joining in on a group in progress feels stupidly daunting to me.

Some people are great at small talk. I find it painful. I can talk to a hairdresser about the weather or my next holiday for exactly five minutes before I have to bury myself in a magazine for the duration of the appointment. I much prefer one-on-ones than group gatherings. I've received incredulous reactions when I've declined invitations for girls' nights out or weekends away. No one can figure out why I wouldn't want to join in on the fun.

For years I didn't understand it either. Why was I the only one who didn't find this kind of fun appealing? I prefer to truly connect with just one person at a time and talk about things that really matter to me, rather than engage in gossip or idle chit-chat. Now that I've opened up about it on my blog, I can see that I'm not alone and I've begun to understand it all much better.

I struggled with my introvert/extrovert tendencies for years until I read that introverts re-energise from time alone, whilst extroverts get energy from interacting with people. That really clicked with me. I love spending time with my family and friends and I would certainly define myself as social, but after a while I feel a bit mentally tired and edgy. After some alone time I feel good again. The surprising thing for me was that this extended to my husband and kids too. I get that same edgy feeling spending extended times with my own family. I thought that maternal instincts would override these sorts of tendencies! For me this realisation has meant I try to carve out some regular alone time each day, even just for ten minutes by getting up before everyone else. If I do that I am a much happier, more patient and productive mum, wife and co-worker!

–Beth

I consider myself an extrovert. I don't mind being by myself at all, but I definitely feel more energised when I'm around other people. When I'm around people who fill me with energy and inspiration I feel fantastic, but when I spend time with people who zap my energy, I feel like an introvert as I just want to get away and be by myself.

–Vicki

Have you heard of the Myers–Briggs personality test? Once I took it, I discovered some fresh insights about myself. The results put me in the middle of the introvert-extrovert scale. It definitely depends on the situation and whom I'm with. It turns out that I'm a 'Protagonist: ENFJ' personality, which makes up only two per cent of the population and explains my desire to want to lead others and myself to a brighter future.

You can take a free online personality test at www.16personalities.com.

Here's what some mothers have said after seeing their results:

It taught me so much about myself and how I relate to others; also getting to know other people that have a similar personality to mine made me feel less of a weirdo. As an INFJ, I'm the most rare and complex personality type – one per cent of the population! It's a really fun thing to do and helps to find out about other people around you too.

—Irene

I'm a big believer in this test. My husband and I did it as marriage prep and discovered we're complete opposites. It helps me (in particular) to know how to approach him about things and how he handles and reacts to situations. For years we struggled to understand each other; now it's much more harmonious.

—Liz

I don't always feel like a 'fun' person but I've come to realise after taking the test that as an introvert I often have a different idea of fun than others who like lots of socialising. Fun to me can be a cosy hour on the couch with my cat and a good book or a family movie night. I'm also part of a book club which meets every six weeks.

—Jan

The test results can be helpful in understanding yourself better so you can practise more self-compassion and have confidence in your strengths. It also provides insight into what your personality type is like as a parent.

Be a Student for Life

Worried that your cogs are turning rusty and want to get your brain in learning mode again? I consider myself a student for life who'll always want to learn about new things. I'm not academically inclined and am more interested in learning about things I can apply to my everyday life.

I did a course in positive thinking at a local yoga centre that really helped my state of mind in the early baby stages. When my kids were very young I did The Parent Practice course to learn practical parenting skills – which continue to be invaluable to me as a mother. Once my kids started school I did a yoga teacher training course for the fun of it – and became a yoga school drop-out just before I was due for my final assessment! Much later I enrolled in an online business school. I've also taken a photography course and Spanish classes – way before I ever knew I'd be moving to Spain and desperately needing it. *(If only I'd taken it more seriously.)*

I now run online courses for mothers because I know how fun it is to log on to a course, watch videos, read content and complete homework assignments that can be immediately applied to everyday life. It gets you thinking in new ways and helps you solve problems and brainstorm solutions – plus it's fun to engage with other like-minded mamas in the course membership group.

Here's what some of my course participants have said about their experiences:

Even though it was all done over the internet, I felt very connected to the group. I loved the worksheets – habits, daily planning, weekly review, monthly review, setting goals and breaking them down, choosing which goals to focus on. Having all of this covered created an easy structure. It gave me the tools to find clarity amongst the chaos and I kept motivated to stay on top of it all.
–Ursula

This is my very first online learning experience and you've made it feel very personal. I enjoyed your videos, the expert contributors, and support and accountability in a safe and private place.
–Sam

This course came along just at the right time for me – I now feel empowered to get things done. I've enjoyed carvng out time for myself and I feel that I have the tools, mindset and support network I need to keep on moving forward.
–Julie

An internet search will bring up a huge array of online courses that you can do from the comfort of home and around your family commitments. Explore local in-person courses too where you can get out of the house and interact with other adults with the same interests.

Family Fun

Are you having enough fun together as a family? Whether you're a single mother with one child, or married with several children, doing fun things together is bonding. Family fun can take place indoors with board games, movie nights, pizza Friday or Saturday night disco, or outdoors with nature adventures, sightseeing, local events or weekends away. It's tricky when family members don't all have the same idea of fun, so attempt to balance the activities so everyone gets a shot at what they'd like to do. It's a great way to demonstrate compromise and they may just surprise themselves by having a great time.

> *As a family we look for a fun yearly theme. Last year it was sport – we researched loads of different sporting activities, going to watch, participating, following a football team in a different country. We extended this out to playing sports video games together too. This year our family theme is 'With the Dog' so we can do more fun things with our new puppy, like pub walks in the countryside.*
> **–Sam**
>
> *We love the freedom of not owning a dog, but get to dogsit regularly by hosting through a wonderful UK agency called Barking Mad. It's great fun getting to know all the different breeds and individual personalities. Thoroughly recommend. We have fun taking the dogs out for long walks in the woods as a family.*
> **–Sherry**

Parent and child yoga is always a thumbs-up in our house! 'Flying' (acro yoga) with daddy and before bedtime my son and I like to do hand mudras (symbolic hand gestures of joy and happiness).
—Natalie

We have fun playing board games and watching films, then talking about them.
—Debz

Two of our family favourites for letting off steam before bedtime are the Sock Game: we all have to try and get each other's socks off, sometimes in teams, sometimes individually; and the Pillow Game: the kids put pillows and cuddly toys in a big pile on the floor and have to try and throw them all onto our bed, while we keep throwing them off . . . Whoever gets them all on/off the bed wins! Both games always end up with lots of laughter!
—Sarah

Get your own family brainstorming about more ways to have fun together.

Fun with Friends

My ever-positive grandma Millie gave me some excellent advice when I got married. She told me that no matter how loved-up I was: **'Never forget about your girlfriends!'** She outlived two husbands and always had her girlfriends for support and companionship. Those gals knew how to have a **fun** time. They got together regularly to play cards or Scrabble, went off on outings and adventures, and even went on a camping trip in their eighties! They kept their sense of humour and teased each other relentlessly. Grandma Millie's very best friend passed away one day before she did. Both asked after the other in their final moments, neither knowing that the other was dying in a separate hospital bed. They'd been friends for eighty-eight years.

When I do my Project Me Life Wheel® assessment every month I hear my grandmother's wise words in my ear as I mark the Fun and Friendships area of my life. If I haven't connected with some of my most cherished friends for a while, it's my nudge to do so. Friendships need a degree of consistency and regularity to keep them going strong – even when we're busy. Here we are in the age of faster, 'better' communication than ever before with phones that are attached to us at all times, yet we're often too busy to reach out for anything other than a text or quick social media comment. *I'm very guilty of this.*

Consider opportunities to do a friend-errand combo. Meet a friend at a nail bar for a catch-up while you dry, have a weekly workout date, plan a joint Ikea trek and catch up over some Swedish meatballs midway through the maze. It'll give you both a real 'ticked off two boxes at once' feeling. Combining your friends and your kids is another great idea. Your child is more likely to value friendships if they see you engaging in them, so make a point of organising a get-together that includes kids too.

Know that there are different types of friendships and we need them in different ways

Some friendships are **casual** – you may be connected through school or your local community and chat about more general things. The more consistently you see these casual friends the more of a chance there is of developing a deeper friendship, but not necessarily and that's OK. Having a familiar face to chat to at work, at the school gates, children's birthday parties and sports events gives us a sense of safety and support. We may be able to call on them for a favour and reciprocate when they need one.

Other friendships are **deep and intimate** – you know everything about each other's struggles and dreams, you make room for each other, you have a strong bond that remains even if you no longer live nearby or see each other as often as you'd like.

There are many friendships that fall somewhere in between casual and intimate or fluctuate between the two at different times in your life. You might have friends you haven't seen in a long time, but when you get together you're able to pick up right where you've left off. Or you may feel you don't have as much in common with someone who used to be a close friend. It's natural for friendships to shift throughout life. Some friendships serve different purposes at different times.

Take Action!

Make a list of all of your friends. Create a mind map to show where friendships intersect. Use your list as a reference when planning social get-togethers or reconnecting with friends you haven't caught up with for a long time. Don't be too busy to reach out and keep the connection strong. When you move into the later chapters in your life, you'll be happy you did.

Friendship Challenges

Are there any specific friendship issues that are dragging you down? Whether it's an open conflict, unsaid words, or a general feeling of wanting to disentangle from a friendship, it's tricky to figure out what to do.

> *I have a friendship I don't find positive for many, many reasons. I've been trying for ten years to drop the friendship. I've managed to disentangle as much as I can without actually saying I'd rather not have any relationship at all but she still contacts me, invites me to stay/meet up, etc. I feel awful as I know she'd be really upset if I was honest but I'm constantly making excuses and avoiding her. I read lots of comments on Facebook etc. about weeding friendships but it's not always quite that easy. (Or is it?!?!?)*
> **—Kate**
>
> *I had a group of school mums who regularly met for coffee. They were often bitchy about others and every time I met with them I felt terrible and would often carry this feeling with me for the rest of the day. I felt talked across, unimportant and not good enough. I suddenly realised how stupid it was to put myself in this position. I just stopped having anything to do with them as a group and sought out other people. I've never regretted that decision and will never put myself in that position again!*
> **—Katrina**

I avoid dramas like the plague and gossip gives me the creeps. These are values I hold very dearly as I want to show up as my authentic self in my friendships, without fear of judgement or being the subject of gossip or backhanded compliments. I've had to distance myself from some friendships that were repeatedly affecting my happiness.

All peace must begin with yourself. The more you get to know and understand yourself, the easier it is to recognise your own imperfections and to accept the imperfections of others.

This is **not** permission to stay in abusive relationships or to put up with damaging behaviours. We need to establish firm boundaries with people who continually hurt us. It's also acceptable to avoid people who repeatedly exhaust us. We only have so much energy to give and we need to give that energy to those we value the most in our lives – especially ourselves.

If the friendship means something to you, it's worth digging deeper into how they are triggering you and what can be done to make things better. If the friendship is more fleeting and circumstantial (mothers from your child's school or someone you work with, for example), begin to distance yourself in a peaceful, kind way by simply being less available and without invoking any drama over it. Turn to the Personal Growth chapter for inspiration to be your best self in all situations.

Friendships can be tricky to navigate, but there are some great Fun and Friendships resources at the back of this book to help give you a fresh perspective.

peace

not drama

Journal Prompt

★ What frustrates me the most in my friendship with _____?

★ What role does blame, jealousy, judgement, non-reciprocation or neglect play in this?

★ What does this friend do or say that triggers me?

★ Does this say more about her or me?

★ What have I already tried to do to make things better?

★ What did or didn't work?

★ What's my Dream Vision of how I'd love my friendship with _____ to look and feel?

★ How will I feel when that Dream Vision is my reality?

★ What could happen if I simply do nothing?

★ What are one to three small-step actions I can take to improve things?

Now write those actions on an Ideas Into Action Sheet – and get moving on them. You'll be so happy you did.

Make New Friends

Are you lacking meaningful friendships? Do you miss having friends you can confide in? Or ones you can let your hair down with and just have a good laugh? Maybe you've moved somewhere new and are starting all over again with making local friends?

Great friendships may have felt easier to come by when you were younger. Once you have kids it's easy to get caught up in family life and let old friendships take a back seat. In many cases jobs take us away and replant us in new places where the process of making local friends means starting over from scratch.

Experts say that friendship has an even greater effect on health than a spouse or family member. Having strong social bonds is probably the most meaningful contributor to happiness and those who have supportive friends are more likely to lose weight, get a new job or pursue their goals. It's not just a matter of waiting long enough until you discover the right person. **You need to get proactive.**

As an adult I've had three major life relocations and know what it's like to start over with finding new friends. Each time I feared I'd never form friendships as close as the ones I'd left behind, yet each time I was wrong. My old Girl Scout motto rings true: 'Make new friends, but keep the old. One is silver and the other's gold.'

MAKE NEW FRIENDS

BUT KEEP THE OLD

ONE IS

silver

AND THE OTHER'S

gold

- Girl Scout Motto -

I'm grateful to have read *Friendships Don't Just Happen: The Guide to Creating a Meaningful Circle of Girlfriends* by friendship expert Shasta Nelson at the perfect time in my life. I was living in Madrid and struggling with the way expat friends were always moving away as soon as we'd grown close. I found myself retreating rather than putting myself out there to meet new friends. Within two days of reading Shasta's book I made two amazing new friends!

Shasta points out that we often write people off without really getting to know them. We assume they're not our type or we won't have anything in common because they don't have kids or don't have a child a similar age to ours – or we assume they wouldn't be interested in us. The potential to meet a new friend is always there if you keep an open mind.

I've made great friends in all kinds of places, from sitting next to each other in a nail bar, to sitting beside each other on an airplane. I even made a dear friend after stopping her on the street to ask where she got her shoes! When she offered to loan them to me, I knew she was something special.

Here are some tips for attracting some new, positive friends in your life:

- Look out for those who give off a positive energy. You can see it in their face and body language. In the local playground or cafe, at the school gates, at the gym, in your yoga class.
- Be aware of your own 'vibe' and what you're giving off. Is your body language closed or open? Are you frowning or smiling? How do you think you may come across to other people as a first impression?
- Strike up a conversation. Compliment them and ask where they got that great scarf/pair of shoes/yoga mat. Ask if they know where you could find a good orthodontist/hairdresser/babysitter. Or tell them about the new find *you* just discovered. A potential new friend will welcome your initiative and want to engage with you.
- Share enough to feel honest and show that you're willing to go beyond surface subjects, but be aware that friendships have to move through stages naturally. Don't unload your entire life story in one sitting or dump your problems on someone you've not yet established trust with. Some friendships naturally develop into a place of sharing vulnerabilities over time.
- Be the friend you'd like to have. Be interested. Listen and talk in equal measure.

Exchange information. Follow up.

- Meaningful friendships take time and consistency to evolve. If you click with someone, but then don't see them with enough regularity, you won't move through the necessary stages. Don't always wait for them to call you – or be too busy when they reach out. Be proactive, make time, stay connected.

The adage is true: you can't choose your family but you can choose your friends. Even with limited time and energy you can take small steps to seek out the support groups you need and spend time with friends that nourish you in different ways.

Don't sit back and wait for others to come to you. Set an intention to make new friends, then take inspired action. See the Fun and Friendships resources (page 290) for lots of ideas, then use an Ideas Into Action Sheet to take one to three small-step actions.

I SURROUND MYSELF WITH PEOPLE WHO LIFT ME

Higher

Create Your Project Me Power Posse

In 2008 I formed a Power Posse with my friends Suzie and Anna. They didn't yet know each other very well but we'd all attended a series of life coaching workshops and wanted a way of keeping on top of the changes we were beginning to make. We were looking for accountability – and *boy* did we find it. We've met up once a month ever since!

In the early days we bumbled along, not quite sure what we were doing, but over time, our sessions developed like a fine wine. Before every meet-up we each do our Project Me Life Wheel® assessment and make some notes about the areas we want to talk about. During the session we take it in turns to share our successes and any challenges we're facing. No matter how busy we are, we carve out time for our monthly mastermind because we know the investment gives a huge payoff. We leave each session feeling fired up and focused. It's amazing to feel so in control of our lives – *instead of life controlling us.* Our Power Posse is the driving force that sparked the idea for Project Me.

Consider getting together with a friend regularly for the 'soul' purpose of goal setting, brainstorming and supporting each other through life's ups and downs. It's one of the most positive ways to take action, find accountability and move forward in life. This can take place in person over a coffee, or online using Skype, Google Hangouts or FaceTime. See the Fun and Friendships resources for the Project Me Power Pal Pack – a guide and workbook to help you create your own Power Posse.

I'm really enjoying my monthly Skype chat with Julia and find it really helpful going through the different aspects of the Life Wheel. It's great to have an outlet and confidential sounding board that's separate from family life and friends.

It's funny that we both met originally when our children were at nursery together nine years ago, but didn't realise how much we had in common until we met again through Project Me when I'd moved many miles away! I'm working on Money and Health (exercise and mindfulness) and Julia has made some great suggestions. We've booked our sessions for the next few months ahead and have committed to reading The Secret *before our next one.*

–Fiona

Take Action!

If you have a friend or friends in mind for forming a Power Posse but aren't sure if they'd be up for it/have time/be the right fit – simply tell them about it and ask them what they think. It's the most proactive first step you could possibly take and you won't know until you ask!

For printable copies of the Fun Seeker, Ideas Into Action or Challenge Solver Action Sheets, go to www.myprojectme.com/action-sheets.

MY VIBE ATTRACTS MY TRIBE!

money

Money

When the Money area of your life isn't flowing well, there's a danger of it leaching into other areas too. If you feel there's not enough money to have fun, you stop looking for fun and life becomes bland and dry, leaving you *more* time to dwell on it. If you can't afford regular date nights or you're arguing about spending and saving, it may drive a wedge between you and your partner. Money worries can become stressful and all-consuming, affecting your health and wellbeing. You can end up stuck in a hard place.

This chapter is designed to help improve your money mindset while also giving you stronger money skills and resources to help you climb into a better position. As always, it's about taking consistent, small-step actions to improve things and not allowing any setbacks to defeat you.

If you've headed to this section because of the Life Wheel prompt about making a will or knowing where to find key financial documents, these are covered in this chapter too.

Money Mindset

Before diving into the practical side of things, it's important to take a step back and look at your money mindset – the foundation and core of where many money issues lie. Money is a very emotionally charged subject and your relationship with money determines how well it flows. Once you get into a mindset of 'lacking', it's a self-fulfilling prophecy. You can't afford the things that would make you happier, which makes you more unhappy, creating a negative, downward spiral.

Your money mindset began forming when you were a child. What do you remember your parents saying about money when you were growing up? Maybe they said things like, 'We can't afford that' or 'It's too expensive'. Perhaps you overheard them criticising a neighbour for buying a 'flashy' car or a relative for 'bragging' about their promotion. This kind of talk can lead to scarcity beliefs (not having 'enough') or fears that success will make you less of a nice person. If your parents divorced you may have found yourself in the middle of arguments and battles over money. Subconscious money memories show themselves as envy, fear, worry, anxiety and overwhelm around money-related matters. They go on to form money blocks – financial obstacles that actually stop you from living the life of abundance that you were meant to lead.

My family didn't have a lot of money when I was growing up. There was always food on the table and shoes on our feet and if I wanted something my parents never said, 'We can't afford it' – they just told me to ask for it on my birthday or put it on my Christmas list, probably hoping that by then I'd forget about it. We only went to a restaurant for special occasions and I had exactly two holidays in my entire childhood – both were long drives in the car. I flew in an airplane for the first time when I was twenty-one. I made money from babysitting, delivering newspapers, cleaning houses and waitressing. I understood the value of money because I had to earn it. I won my first prize draw in a raffle when I was a young child and my grandfather dubbed me his 'lucky charm'. From that day forward I've always entered competitions – and often I win. My money mindset from a young age was: 'I'm a winner!'

A painful childhood memory was of my mother telling me that she was going to start doing the night shift in the factory where she worked. She wouldn't be home when I returned from school or to put me to bed. I cried as she explained she was doing it to earn more money so we could afford to buy a bigger house. My life was the same as every other kid I knew, so it came as a real shock. She described the new house we'd live in and how I'd have my own bedroom and together we looked at a sales catalogue so I could choose a new bedspread and matching curtains. The truth is, having my mother there when I came home from school was more important to me than having my own bedroom, but I can see now, as a parent myself, that there were probably other decisions that they were considering.

Once we moved into the bigger house we were in a more affluent area, and when I got to my new school my clothes were all wrong and I felt like I didn't fit in. My mother continued to work the night shift to keep up with the expenses, and eventually she and my step-dad divorced. I looked after my brother and myself since she wasn't home after school and was still asleep in the mornings. She was never there for my school ceremonies or performances and I always had to ask someone else's parents for a ride home afterwards. I started ducking out of the back and making the long walk home by myself after dark to avoid the shame of it.

I couldn't wait to move out and I paid my own way through university with scholarship money, loans, cleaning jobs and working at a dry cleaner's. I fully appreciate what it's like to have no savings and to live off Pot Noodles, yet somehow I never adopted a money mindset of 'lack'. I had big plans of moving to California to work behind the scenes in Hollywood and once I actually started living the 'California Dream', my furniture was from garage sales and my car was second-hand. I always felt grateful for what I had and I now see that the vibration I was giving out made me a magnet for attracting more abundance into my life.

If I'd been surrounded by loads of toys as a child, went on exotic holidays every summer and was given money for university, maybe I wouldn't have felt as deeply appreciative of the things that money can buy as I am today. If I'd heard my parents complaining about not having 'enough', I may have adopted a scarcity money mindset. Hardships and challenges are there to shape us and I'm appreciative of the lessons I've learned along the way.

I wish
good fortune
and happiness
for myself and
everyone.

My own kids are very privileged with regular holidays, meals out and entertainment. I teach them the value of money by giving them an allowance they earn by helping out around the house. I don't believe kids *need* to be paid to pitch in at home, but once mine reached an age of wanting to buy things – cinema tickets and ice creams with friends, gadgets and clothes beyond the essentials – it made sense for them to earn their own spending money, rather than handing it to them whenever they wanted something. It also taught them how to save and keep track of money. I gently encourage a mindset of gratitude and my older son and I have a morning ritual of putting our hand on our heart and thinking of whatever we're feeling grateful for that day.

Somehow I've made it through life without any major money blocks and abundance flows freely for me. If that stirs up any negative feelings towards me or yourself, recognise that this is a mindset that blocks you from receiving. If it makes you feel happy for me or inspired for yourself, you're in a state of allowing. Notice your mindset around other people you know. Once you are truly happy for other people's wealth and success, you'll allow abundance to flow into your own life.

Your Money Blocks

Releasing your personal money blocks means recognising the thought patterns that aren't serving you, working through those feelings and getting to the other side of your glass ceiling. Become aware of when they're creeping in to try to sabotage you. Listen out for that voice that says things like:

'I don't deserve it.'
'That'll never happen for me.'
'I could only ever dream of having that.'
'If only.'
'I'll just have to settle with what I've got.'

Notice too the thoughts you have about other people's financial success:

'Must be nice for some.'
'She clearly married him for the money.'
'If I had the money they did, I sure wouldn't spend it on that.'
'He's got more money than sense.'

Or you might find yourself comparing yourself to someone else:

'I never dress as well as she does.'
'He always treats his wife to nice things.'
'If only I could be jetting off on *my* fourth holiday of the year.'
'I'll never be able to throw a birthday party like this for my child.'

Judging others is toxic, even when you mentally come out on top. Comparisons undermine your own sense of self-worth.

Every time you notice yourself in a mindset of 'lack of' or 'not enough', shift your mind to one of abundance. Say affirmations like: 'I am a money magnet!', 'I can always get what I want', 'I'm open to receiving', 'Money flows freely to me', 'I live an abundant life'.

I have a tough time spending money on myself. I'm trying to overcome this issue because it really gets in the way of me getting regular massages and other small treats. For instance, right now I could really stand to buy a new pair of jeans and a few shirts but I'll probably drag my feet a few weeks longer. And my makeup supply needs a serious overhaul but I seem stuck on the expense of it all. A lot of it is due to how I was raised money-wise, but my husband and I also had a couple of tough years financially so it's been somewhat difficult for me to get comfortable having money again.

–Bambi

MAMA MANTRA

money flows freely to me

#PROJECTME

MAMA MANTRA:

I AM GRATEFUL FOR ALL OF THE MONEY I HAVE RECEIVED IN MY LIFE.

#ProjectMe

An Attitude of Gratitude

A great way to keep the flow of abundance coming to you in life is to practise an attitude of gratitude. If we don't fully appreciate what we have, we limit the flow of abundance.

Here's a little money 'trick' I use every time I withdraw cash. During that pause while the machine is counting out the notes I give a silent thank you and feel gratitude that I can walk up to a hole in the wall and pull out cold hard cash. I mean, how amazing is that? There are billions of people in the world who could only dream of this, yet most of us do it so mechanically that we don't even think about how wondrous this is. As the little slot opens and the cash reaches your hands, feel a wave of gratitude.

It's these moments of receiving money that we need to notice, appreciate and feel grateful for. It doesn't matter if you're overdrawn, you feel underpaid or that the money is going straight towards paying a bill or the taxman – negative feelings about money push it further away from you, while an attitude of gratitude attracts it.

If that all sounds a bit too 'woo-woo' for you, here it is from a more logical perspective. Whatever you give more attention grows. When you're clear about what you want and you put energy into getting it, it's far more likely to happen than sitting around complaining about it, right?

Upgrading

Even if you don't have all of the money you desire yet, treat yourself to lifestyle upgrades that make you *feel* abundant. Money mindset coach Denise Duffield-Thomas has a fun and insightful exercise where you look at a variety of items you own and assess whether they're first-class or economy.

Is your underwear first-class or economy? I don't actually like fancy pants, but once I assessed my undie drawer I spotted a lot of economy rubbish in there that had to go. Now I always find what I want without rummaging through all of the crappy stuff.

The same thing happened when I assessed our bedding. I'd been craving some luxurious Egyptian cotton sheets, but I always baulked at the cost. I then found an online shop and subscribed to their newsletter to get 20 per cent off my first purchase. I got a few things and then, whenever there was a sale, I'd top up with another piece. Over time I got two complete sets so when one's in the laundry we aren't back to the old stuff. I finally splashed out on a mattress topper and now our bed is so freaking luxurious it feels like sleeping in a five star hotel! That is what I call a first-class upgrade.

Even small things like upgrading wire hangers to wooden ones makes my clothes feel like they've been given a first-class upgrade. I bought wooden hangers from Ikea, a dozen at a time, and gave the wire hangers to my local dry cleaner's.

If you've got chipped crockery, holey socks, a rug that keeps tripping you up – it can make you feel like you're living an economy life. Look for small ways to upgrade to first class and it'll shift your financial energy. And remember: it's not selfish to spend money on yourself.

One of the things I've learned is that we tend to look at money and abundance just in terms of cash, but actually this is not the case. We need to take account of many things, like freebies, discounts, scholarships, vouchers, bonus points (like in the supermarket), air miles, favours from friends, presents, etc. Abundance and money come to us in very many shapes and forms, and we need to be grateful and aware for it to multiply even further!

—**Irene**

I deserve to live an

abundant life!

Living By Your Values

We live in a 'buy, buy, buy' society – and it starts with the new pram. The baby doesn't care about the new pram; it just wants to be held. This pattern of spending money continues throughout their childhood. Our children would much rather we play a game together than buy them something. It's the time spent with us they crave. We don't think we have the energy or time to sit down and play a game, yet if we value communication and connection with our child, even a regular five-minute game of Go Fish or dominos will create an important anchor.

Many children's birthday parties are over-the-top and some parents feel under pressure to spend more than they can afford. Goodie bags, personalised cakes, balloons, face-painting, entertainment, bouncy castles, catering – children's birthday parties have become big business. We're all susceptible to comparisons of what their classmates are doing and getting sucked into the consumerism trap of what we think we need to do to make our child feel special on their birthday. Google 'How to make my child feel special on their birthday' and you'll find loads of creative, sweet, inexpensive and free ideas. Your child will feel genuinely special on their birthday when you shower them with extra love and attention, and you're teaching them the value of what's truly important in life.

We already know that money doesn't buy happiness, so we need to make choices and compromises to find a balance that fits in with our values.

Many years ago, when anxiety over job security got too much, we decided that our absolute priority would be to pay off our mortgage. To live comfortably within our means, to save up to buy things, to plan to have enough money to have fun, and to communicate clearly with each other about money. Our life decisions are based around these principles or philosophies.

We have never felt the need to compete or prove our worth. I observe this behaviour with acquaintances and it truly baffles me. It's not about which car I drive, the size of my home, the labels on my clothes, the holiday destinations – these don't define my character or my heart! I feel very grateful for our 'wealth', but I don't measure this solely in money.

–Samantha

Money Concerns

If you have serious money worries that are niggling away at your happiness or keeping you up at night, it's not just a case of thinking positive and hoping it'll all get better on its own. This is where you need to combine mindset with action. The first step is to change the word 'worry' to 'concern'.

Make a list of any of your concerns in the Money area of your life. Notice the unrealistic fears that are very unlikely to ever happen. Catastrophising is an irrational way of thinking or believing that something is far worse than it actually is. Cross those out – or write them on a piece of paper and burn them!

Now you're left with the concerns that are perhaps more realistic. By breaking these down and creating a small-step action plan, you can stop being paralysed and move yourself forward. Having messy finances is stressful. Maybe you need to get some systems in place to make you feel more in control and on top of it all.

Make paying off any debts a priority. Debt is like a straitjacket that carries a weight that spreads into all other life areas. It's a heavy burden to bear, so acknowledge this and be gentle but firm with yourself about taking baby steps towards paying off the one that has the smallest balance. Emotionally, as women, once we feel a sense of progress, we can then move forward.

Money Goals

Move your finances forward with clear, written goals and a plan of action. Your plan doesn't need to be a long, detailed, hashed-out masterpiece. Simply write down one to three first steps you could take to get you off the starting blocks. This builds momentum and it gets easier from there.

When I work with mothers to set goals, we always begin by visualising the result they're after. How would this area of their life look, feel and be if they'd given it a high score? After a detailed brain-dump on paper they get behind their 'why' – WHY do they want this? They then create a Hot Power Statement that sums up their vision using positive, present-tense language – as if their Dream Vision is already their reality.

Jill, a mother of two running her own childcare business, did my goal-setting course. She marked the Money area of her life low, saying:

It's time to get my s**t together and act like a grown-up! I want to take my business to the next level so I've decided to focus on Money.

Jill's Hot Power Statement:

I am responsible with spending and saving wisely. I make smart decisions to keep my family and our businesses safe from unforeseen expenses.

I told Jill I thought that was great – except that 'unforeseen expenses' is negative language and calls to mind what she doesn't want. Our minds latch on to the language we use, so it's important to focus on what we do want. Jill tweaked her Hot Power Statement to:

I am a smart and powerful CEO, taking my business to the next level. I spend and save wisely and make clever decisions that bring financial abundance to my family.

Much more powerful! Think about this when setting your own goals and creating your own Hot Power Statement. Jill later shared her success story with me:

I had a breakthrough with my goal and it felt great. I began to save money monthly in a hidden account that I don't have access codes to. My husband and I are both self-employed and our companies are in large growth phases, which requires sacrifices in financial areas. January came around and we had a lack of liquidity in both of our companies. Our children's school tuition was due and my husband called in a panic. I surprised him and told him about the money I'd saved. He was so happy and proud of me! It took a huge weight off both of our shoulders to be able to pay everything off in full. I felt empowered and responsible.

Defining Your Money Management Roles

'The Money Coach' Julie Feuerborn encourages us to think of our household as being **the family business** of raising kids. The most successful businesses have one person as CEO (chief executive officer) and another as CFO (chief financial officer) – they work together to share responsibility for the growth of the family business.

Julie says, 'Once somebody has been cast in the role as CFO, by default the other person then becomes the CEO. As CEO you may be the person that does the grocery shopping, pays bills, buys school shoes, etc. – so you're still the financial manager on those levels – but the CFO keeps track of the big picture planning.'

Julie encourages parents to have a monthly board meeting about their family. These meetings don't have to be formal and stuffy. If there's tension around money, you need to go into it with a business hat on and with the mindset of both parents working for the best way to run their family business.

When you have those meetings and the CFO is being controlling about money or the CEO doesn't have access to accounts like the other one does, the CEO has permission to say, 'Let's talk about how that money is being spent.' It removes the emotion on some level because you're putting that business hat on. It opens the opportunity to discuss where the family is headed. What's important to this family? Is that new car important, or would it be better spent on something else? A family adventure? Education? It's a chance to have a good conversation about family values and what's important in the long and short terms.

Joint Accounts and Expenses

How do you pay for joint expenses in your household? Does it all come out of a shared account, or do you hold separate accounts and keep track of expenses?

My husband and I opened a joint account after we got married. He sees me as his equal share partner in running our family and home and trusts me, so all money is 'our' money and all expenses come out of our joint account. Even when I haven't been earning much (or any) money, there are never any issues over fairness. Other couples keep their money separate. Money is exceptionally personal and each couple needs to find their best fit. It's about communication and knowing there are options for how to manage money.

> We agree who pays what and we transfer funds to each other as appropriate. We don't share expenses that aren't household/bills/food and use a joint credit card for shopping that we pay off in full each month. We both work full-time and there is unfairness . . . I tend to buy treats and things for our daughter . . . my other half doesn't think to do the same!
> **—Tania**

> I tend to pay for all joint things and then claim the money back from hubby. On his payday, I present him with a grand total of what he owes me that month. When I worked full-time (pre-children) I earned more than he did so I

tended to pay for 'treats' (meals out, cinema, etc.). Now I work part-time we've reversed and he pays for those things.

—Catherine

We had separate accounts for a long time with a joint account for bills but unequal incomes ended up in conversations like who was 'paying for' dinner and it didn't feel like an equal partnership. Now we have a joint account for everything and both pay our salary into it. It feels more liberating and equal even though the money going in reflects the difference in our career situations and my decision to have my own business and be responsible for kids. We have a good, open relationship about money and it feels so much better than the old way.

—Claire

As an expat 'trailing spouse', I resigned my job in a top consulting firm to move abroad yet AGAIN. I asked my husband to make sure that when his package was being negotiated there would be sufficient room to compensate my salary every month. I know we're lucky that our family expatriation is well compensated for, so every month the salary that I let go when I resigned my job is deposited into my personal account. I spend that money on my family and myself as I would if I had received it from my employer, but the fact that it's mine and reflective of my business worth reminds me that I'm not less than I was when I held my job. It gives me an empowered feeling of independence and freedom.

My husband is not hung up on money and we very rarely argue about finances, so it's not that I have any particular reason to do this, other than I MUST do it for ME.

—Sanne

Budgeting, Financial Management and Saving

There's **no one way** to save, budget and track your finances. Some people are really into budgeting, others aren't. There's no right or wrong. I was curious to know how a professional money coach manages her money, so I turned to Julie Feuerborn to see how she and her family do it.

I think budget is a word that makes you think about what you have to 'give up'. I prefer to think of the money as going into different pots. It's important to have a purpose for the money that comes into your life.

I start by knowing what our big regular expenses are, such as the mortgage, utilities, insurances – some are annual, others quarterly or monthly. Since these are all non-negotiable expenses that we have no control over, we have one pot (a current account) that holds the money to cover these regular expenses, which are paid out by direct debit. I check on it, but I don't have to think about it much.

Then there's another pot (a different current account) for all other expenses. That's the one to look at. We're creatures of habit and tend to spend roughly the same amount on food each month, but maybe one month more gets spent on extras. I look at how much needs to be in that account to keep things ticking along each month on average. We don't have to budget per se, we just need to deposit enough into that account to cover expenses and can cut back if that pot is looking depleted.

Then there's the savings account pot for short-term savings that I'll want access to in less than five years. This is for holidays, Christmas spending and our emergency fund.

My favourite account is the long-term investing account for big dreams such as higher education for our children and retirement. Any extra money goes into this account. When salaries go up, this pot gets bigger without even touching it because I've only fed the pots that I need every month. If it comes into my current account, I'm going to spend it. It's human nature.

To make it all work my husband and I deposit money into a separate current account each month and then it all gets distributed from there. It takes a little time to get it organised and set up, but I can tell you that it works. I only have to spend about fifteen minutes each month managing the money.

You need to structure it according to what's important to you and your family. Automate all of your bills so you don't have to worry about them, then distribute your incoming money accordingly. It's not about budgeting, it's about being aware of how you spend and what you want to save for.

Julie stressed that her system isn't the ONLY system and there is no perfect way. Each person and family needs to come up with what works for them. Having clear goals and being conscious about where money goes are the biggest priorities. The rest can fall into place.

Wills and Important Documents

None of us wants to think about the *worst-case scenario*, but burying our heads in the sand leaves us vulnerable. Knowing where important documents and bank account details are kept is a practical consideration and having a will is essential when you have a child or children.

My husband and I spent too many years saying, 'We must do our wills' – but neither of us took any action. When I finally admitted this to a friend I got a huge telling off about how irresponsible we were being. She told me that if we died without a will, the law would decide who gets what, our house would go to the government, our bank accounts would be frozen and no one left behind would have a clue what our wishes are for the children. *Gulp.* It was the lecture I needed to contact a local law firm and ask them how to get started.

Many parents put off making a will because they can't decide on a guardian. Skip thinking about that part for now and simply take the first small step, and then the next one after that without thinking of the whole big picture.

I've since learned that will writers tend to be less expensive than going to a solicitor. Some will writers are former solicitors who are now work-at-home mothers. They will understand how emotional all of this is and can lead you through it gently. Sara Esler of Estate Planning Solutions is one of these mama will writers. She advises, 'Please don't bury your head in the sand when it comes to making a will. It takes just over an hour for you to give instructions and about seven working days for a draft to be issued. It's only a small piece of your time and will save years of heartache for your children and partner.' The Institute of Professional Willwriters' members and associates follow a code of practice approved by Trading Standards. This means that all clients have the same high-quality service provided to them and members and associates are fully insured. They'll visit you in your own home at a time to suit you.

When it comes to knowing where important documents are kept, it's a case of blocking out some time to sit down, list them all, then locate the relevant details and file it all in one place. If all of this feels scary and you want to run away, think of it as a gift to your family. The focus isn't on tragedy; it's a way for you to take care of the ones you love the most. Add it to your Ideas Into Action Sheet and take charge of getting things moving.

Money Leaks

Most people are simply unaware of how much money they spend on the small everyday things. Some of these 'money leaks' could be plugged with a sense of awareness of how we're spending.

Self-made millionaire and author David Bach describes the small amounts we spend here and there as the Latte Factor®. He says if we added up the cost of our daily lattes and saved it or invested it, we could build up wealth significantly faster.

At the risk of sounding like a total freak, I have a confession to make. I've never had a cup of coffee in my life. I don't like the smell of it and have never even fancied a taste. But here's my point: had I been buying myself a couple of coffees a day over the past thirty years I'd have spent something like £55,000 on coffee. Wow! I think I deserve a yoga retreat in some far-flung destination with some of the money I've saved . . .

Whether you want to cut back on your daily caffeine fix or not, being more aware of your money leaks could help you save more. We tend to disregard how quickly little purchases add up over the course of a month.

Common money leaks include: paying for gym memberships you don't use, delivery charges for online purchases, extra banking fees that could be avoided, instantaneous Kindle book purchases (instead of checking the library first), excessive magazines, snacks and sweets your kids manipulate you for at the check-out. These seemingly small spends all add up. Pay attention to the small money leaks so they don't turn into floods.

Tracking Spending

Tracking how you spend your money can be a helpful way of uncovering hidden money leaks and plugging those holes. It also gives you a hard look at yourself and what you really want out of life. It can become the call to action you need to spend less money on the things that don't really matter and save for things that do.

I like to track spending for specific purposes. One year I used a dedicated notebook to write down everything we spent on food. Whenever I came back from a supermarket shop, I'd jot the total in the notebook. If my husband picked up a few things on his way home, he'd hand over the receipt and I'd add it in. As I food shopped I was more aware of throwing things into the basket that weren't worth the price. It gave me the prod I needed to be more mindful and aware.

Another time I tracked money spent on beauty, hair and skincare products. I had a feeling it was a lot and after a few months I was quite appalled. It gave me a reality check that I was falling into the consumerism trap of thinking I had to have whatever I was reading about in the magazines. I made a pact with myself to finish all of what I had without buying more until something ran out and I felt a *genuine* need to replace it. It changed me. I never went back to excessive cosmetic buying again and even now I will painfully endure mascara I don't like before I'll buy another.

When we decided to try a car-free life after our move to London with our teen-agers, we calculated how much money we used to spend on petrol, insurance, taxes, maintenance, repairs, car washes and parking. We never come close to spending what we would have to run a car and get a lot more exercise.

Think about whether tracking expenditures would help you to be more aware of where your money's going and serve as a possible deterrent to wasting it or as a motivation to save for something special. You may want to track something specific, or track everything you spend. Some people like spreadsheets, others like apps and many prefer the good old pen-and-paper approach.

Overspending

Are you prone to spending more money than you probably should? Is there always something else you want to buy? Are you good at rationalising your purchases to convince yourself or others that you really need them?

Overspending can fill an emotional void in the short term, leaving you feeling empty and guilty soon after. It can also tip you into debt or stop you from making any significant savings for the future.

Suzie, a mother of four and a reformed overspender, describes how shopping was her religion for many years and how she changed her ways:

I understand the thrill of the chase – finding that perfect leather jacket (even though I've already got five), that amazing pair of jeans that make my thighs look skinny and my bum look great (although to everyone else they look exactly the same as all the rest).

But I also know how it feels to be in debt – the sleepless nights, penny pinching and being economical with the financial truth.

Over time I began to see that overspending was just so damn wasteful. It felt empty, a vicious circle of want, desire and unfulfilled need – as well as a colossal waste of time and energy that could be used for something way more productive.

Finally I had a light-bulb moment that flipped my attitude completely. Instead of seeing 'not spending' as 'deprivation' – denying myself all the lovely things I desired – I reframed it as 'wealth creation'. I realised I could use money to create a different kind of wealth – experiences, memories, education, security, connection, simplicity – as opposed to just accumulating more stuff.

Arriving at this realisation wasn't easy. It took a lot of time, stress and soul searching for me to get here. Now not spending money makes me feel abundant rather than deprived. I make a valuable contribution towards the cost of running our home and family. I'm also setting a great example to my children. And I love being able to pay for family trips and holidays, sharing experiences and creating happy memories that have a long-lasting positive effect for all of us.

Tips to spend less and be more money mindful

Keep a spending diary.

Write down every penny you spend. Knowing you have to note down *any* expenditure means you'll think twice before you flash the cash *and* you'll see where you spend unnecessarily. The latte habit, glossy magazines, the weekly take-away . . . reframe these extras as the treats they are rather than an everyday fix.

Increase your awareness.

Download your bank's app into your smartphone and check your account balance daily. The more you check your balance the less you'll splurge. The opposite is also true – the more in the dark you are about your finances, the easier it is to spend irresponsibly.

Visualise your goals.

Knowing *why* you want something makes you more likely to achieve it. So get specific about why you want to spend less. Take a pen and paper and jot down your top four goals.

Be grateful.

Love and appreciate what you already have rather than endlessly lusting after more. True happiness is not about owning more stuff. There's already so much waste in the world. Do you really want to add to it?

Take Action!

Becoming the expert of you in the Money area of your life means understanding your money mindset and finding ways to take control of your finances so you can give this a higher score on your Life Wheel on future audits. What actions will you take to get the ball rolling? Remember, baby steps are better than no steps. Use an Ideas Into Action Sheet or a Challenge Solver Action Sheet.

All Action Sheets can be found at www.myprojectme.com/action-sheets.

BEFORE BUYING ANYTHING ASK YOURSELF:

DO I NEED IT?

DO I ALREADY HAVE SOMETHING SIMILAR OR THAT DOES THE SAME JOB?

CAN I BORROW IT?

CAN I AFFORD IT?

I AM THE PROJECT MANAGER OF MY LIFE

#ProjectMe

Final Words

Dear Amazing Mama,

I hope you've enjoyed our ride together – thank you for joining me on this journey. As you may have guessed by now, this adventure is far from over. Different challenges will continue to present themselves throughout every stage of motherhood and beyond. Your Project Me is ongoing and you'll keep expanding on it for the rest of your life. It is my hope that with these new tools under your belt, you have the kick-start you need to feel in better control of your happiness. You're laying the foundation for your big goals and juicy dreams.

Be the Project Manager of your life

Schedule in your Life Wheel assessment each month to make it a regular habit. Holding all of your Action Sheets in a dedicated folder will help you take your Project Me to the next level. You'll have blank sheets at your fingertips so you can plan and figure things out regularly. Always mark your Action Sheets with the date and you'll be amazed and proud to see your progress over time.

Share your wins

The energy you put in will show up in your life in many wonderful ways. I know BIG things are possible for you and I'm excited to hear your progress. Join the Project Me Facebook group and share your wins – big and small. You'll find support, camaraderie, fun challenges and accountability check-ins to keep you on the straight and narrow. www.facebook.com/myprojectme

Keep going!

Want to take things to the next level? I offer online courses, workshops, retreats, mentoring – and I'm always cooking up fresh ideas to keep you motivated and inspired. Jump onto the Project Me V.I.M. (very important mama) list to be kept in the loop.

www.myprojectme.com

I'm here rooting for you every step of the way!
Positively yours,

HAPPINESS IS...

working on my Project Me

Kelly's Treasure Trove of Tried and Tested Resources

Personal Growth

BOOKS

The Magic by Rhonda Byrne

I've recommended this book to countless people and I love getting their heartfelt thanks for the magic it's brought into their lives. It's a 28-day journey with short chapters and written exercises about good health, relationships, work and money. With each day you'll feel positive changes in your emotions and your life. The results truly are magic!

The Untethered Soul by Michael A. Singer

This book exploded onto the scene after the author's appearance on Oprah's *SuperSoul Sunday* show. You are the main character as you get to know your 'inner roommate' and realise what it's like when they're incessantly talking. Once you become more aware of your self-talk, you can learn how to relax your heart and let go of things that would normally upset you. I turn to this book again and again and always learn something new about myself.

Buddhism for Mothers by Sarah Napthali

Raising small children can often make you feel like you've lost the plot. Sarah is a real mother who shares how the concepts of Buddhist practices can make you a calmer and more connected parent. A reassuring read to pick up anytime you're having a tough day and need a nurturing perspective.

Ask and It Is Given by Esther and Jerry Hicks

If you're familiar with the law of attraction and want practical processes to help you manifest your desires, this book will show you how. You'll discover the role emotions play in your life and how to use them as an internal guidance system. Strong 'woo-woo' warning: only for the exceptionally open-minded.

PODCAST

Happy Mama Movement with Amy Taylor-Kabbaz

Motherhood changes us. Our priorities shift, our definition of success evolves, and we find ourselves questioning our addiction to busy-ness. Who are we now? And can we be the best mamas without completely losing ourselves along the way? The Happy Mama Movement is a collection of interviews and insights with real mamas around the world, reflecting on mindfulness, real connection, and the realities of being a modern-day mama.

APPS

Insight Timer is my all-time favourite meditation app with a vast choice of guided recordings of varying lengths, themes and teachers. It's like reading a few pages from an inspiring personal growth book every day. Join the Project Me for Busy Mothers group within the app where we share our favourite meditations and encourage each other to make meditation a regular practice.

Peace Process is an app that lets you type in the words someone said that have bothered or upset you. It could have been said by a friend, a relative, or a co-worker, or it could be something you told yourself. You are then offered some perspective so you can move beyond it. It's surprisingly effective.

Productivity

BOOKS

The Power of Less by Leo Babauta

Many years ago this book first introduced me to the concept of identifying my three MITs (most important tasks) and doing those first. Leo is a huge advocate of simplifying our lives for better productivity and time management. Follow his Zen Habits blog for topics such as mindfulness, parenting, happiness, motivation, eating healthily and successfully implementing good habits.

The Life-Changing Magic of Tidying by Marie Kondo

I read this book ahead of my major home downsize to help me easily and quickly decide what to keep and get rid of. If it doesn't 'spark joy', out it goes. What makes her method speedy is that instead of de-cluttering room by room, she tackles belongings type by type. It's an international bestseller for good reason. It seems to work for a lot of people, myself included.

APPS

Evernote

Are you still using the standard Notes app that came with your phone? Having to scroll down pages of notes to find the one you're looking for? Forget it! Evernote saves your notes into handy little sub-notebooks. *It's become an extension of my brain.* Whenever a friend recommends a book, film or restaurant, I pop it into that notebook for easy access later. My travel notebook is for inspiration, research, itineraries, passport scans and important documents. Evernote also lets you clip recipes straight from the web and store them in a recipes file. It'll help to dramatically reduce paper clutter in your life. It's easier to familiarise yourself with the desktop version first before syncing it to your phone.

Trello

I've been using Trello for years to keep track of my massive to-do list and break projects down into doable actions. The desktop version gives a visual overview, much like a board filled with Post-it notes that can be swapped around easily for prioritisation. Using Trello as your master to-do list saves you from having to re-write tasks again and again as they get carried over to the next day or week. It syncs to your phone so you can add tasks on the fly. I now teach mothers how to manage their time better with a strategy I devised using this amazing app.

AnyList

Ever arrived at the supermarket only to realise you've left your shopping list at home? This happened to me too often until I discovered the AnyList app. My kids are great at adding items to the list as we need them. It gives them input and makes us all responsible for keeping an eye on things we're running low on (*like toilet paper . . .*). Tap the items while you're shopping and your list becomes smaller as you go. If you've accidently crossed something off, shake your phone and it magically appears again.

Family

WEBSITES

The Parent Practice – Positive Parenting Academy

The Parent Practice single-handedly saved my sanity when my family life was out of control. They've taken the same format of the live parenting course I did and turned it into an online version you can do from anywhere in world, at your own pace from the comfort of home. If you live in London, check out their selection of live workshops and courses too.

www.theparentpractice.com

Dr Kirsty Goodwin is an expert on the impact of technology on children. She's passionate about sharing the latest research and insights into how 'digitalised childhoods' are changing the ways that young children learn, play and develop (without telling parents or educators that they need to ban the iPad, or disconnect the internet). Her website offers practical, evidence-based information about what modern kids really need to thrive both online and offline.

www.drkirstygoodwin.com

PODCAST

Zen Parenting Radio

Presented by a spiritual and emotional mum (Cathy) and a logical and practical dad (Todd), the banter between this husband and wife duo is both highly amusing and informative. You can listen from their website or use the podcast app on your phone while you're doing housework, folding laundry, cooking or driving.

www.zenparentingradio.com

BOOKS

Peaceful Parent, Happy Kids: How to Stop Yelling and Start Connecting by Dr Laura Markham

Dr Laura encourages a more positive and gentle approach to parenting rather than relying on punishment, shouting and threats. This book teaches you how to build a great relationship with your child, whilst setting clear boundaries. Her Aha! Parenting website is pure gold for parents with kids of any age.

www.ahaparenting.com

Real Parenting for Real Kids: Enabling Parents to Bring Out The Best In Their Children by Melissa Hood

Melissa was my first parenting coach at The Parent Practice and my private session with her inspired me to attend the ten-week course that ultimately turned our family life around. Melissa knows her stuff and this book is the second best thing to joining their course.

The Family Virtues Guide: Simple Ways to Bring Out the Best in Our Children and Ourselves by Linda Kavelin Popov

This is a practical how-to manual for instilling good values in your children. Open it up to any page and you'll find one of fifty-two virtues (one for every week of the year), such as caring, compassion, generosity, tolerance and trust – all carefully explained in a language kids can understand and relate to. I'm often complimented on my kids' kindness, respect and self-confidence. This book gave me the framework to help them develop these qualities.

COMMUNICATION GAMES

Fink Conversation Cards

These fun, thought-provoking question cards are designed to get families talking. They're great for starting conversations, learning about each other and helping children to positively improve their communication skills. They're perfect for long car journeys or waiting in restaurants, instead of being glued to technology.
www.finkcards.com

Orchard Toys

These are my absolute favourite for making game-playing fun for small kids and their parents. My kids grew up on these games and learned how to take turns and develop personal and social skills, literacy, numbers, matching and memory skills. I never minded sitting on the floor and playing an Orchard game with them as they are so fun and visually appealing!
www.orchardtoys.com

Health and Wellbeing

WEBSITES

Julie Clark is on a mission to teach families how to eat a healthy diet and lead a healthy life. If you've got a fussy eater or have a family member with allergies or intolerances, Julie's website is full of help. She also has an online course to help mothers with weight loss and health goals.
www.julieclarknutrition.co.uk

Vicky Warr at TheBeezKneez is the go-to expert for strengthening and toning your post-natal tummy and getting back into shape with exercise and nutrition. Her online videos take only twenty minutes a day and she has a reputation for getting great results.
www.beezkneezhive.com

FlexTV allows you to work out from home along with fitness instructors and the support of a community. You can set reminders, get accountability, and choose from a wide variety of classes including cardio, dance, post-natal, toning, yoga, and Pilates at times of the day that suit you.
www.joinflex.tv

MindHealth360 is a free and comprehensive online guide to integrative mental health, offering the latest research and information to help those suffering from common mental health issues (such as depression, anxiety, insomnia poor concentration, poor memory, irritability). It allows you to enter symptoms, see possible causes and find solutions.
www.mindhealth360.info

APP

Aaptiv is an on-demand audio fitness app that combines the guidance of a trainer with the perfect playlist to give you a fresh way to work out. Pop in your ear buds and head outdoors for a run, or jump on one of the cardio machines at the gym. There are also programmes to train for 5K or 10K runs – or even a whole marathon! Check out the website first to see how it all works, then download the app to get started.
www.aaptiv.com

BOOKS

The Headspace Guide to Meditation and Mindfulness by Andy Puddicome

An easy-to-read and understand book about mindfulness and using meditation as a tool to feel more calm and even-tempered, filled with little exercises to help us become more aware of our passing thoughts and emotions without getting caught up and carried away with them. It's a thin, light paperback you can slip into your handbag to read whenever you've got a couple of minutes of waiting time.

Bach Flower Remedies for Beginners by David Vennells

I'm a huge fan of natural flower remedies for treating the emotional ups and downs of my family and me. Flower remedies can be found at chemists and health food stores and the most popular brand is Bach. Bach Rescue Remedy is a saviour to keep in your handbag. Dubbed 'yoga in a bottle', it'll save you from a mama meltdown when the going gets tough. This book serves as my main reference for dosing out the magic potions.

The UltraMind Solution: The Simple Way to Defeat Depression, Overcome Anxiety, and Sharpen Your Mind by Mark Hyman, MD

This book teaches you how to heal your body naturally, making diet and lifestyle changes that will foster brain function, including memory, mood and attention span, as well as anything from brain fatigue to depression.

How to Live Well with Chronic Pain and Illness: A Mindful Guide by Toni Bernhard

This comes highly recommended if you are chronically ill, or a carer of a person who is. With easy-to-learn exercises and many personal stories, you'll find lots of comfort and practical guidance here.

Love

WEBSITES

Isiah McKimmie is a relationship therapist and sexologist who helps individuals and couples improve their sex lives and relationships. Her website and podcast are full of inspiration for how to boost your confidence in the bedroom and find deeper intimacy. www.isiah-mckimmie.com

Maj Wismann is a Danish sexologist who helps women and men to have a better sex life, as well as incorporate more love, closeness and intimacy into their relationships. She

has free online courses and ebooks to dive in and explore.
www.majwismann.com

Julie Marah is a 'wife coach' who'll get you crystal clear on who you are now, what you want for your life *and* your marriage, and how to give yourself permission to create a happy and fulfilling life. If you find yourself wondering, 'Should I stay or should I go?', Julie has great tools to help you decide.
www.juliemarah.com

Summer Howard of Bridge to Bliss is a relationship and divorce coach who does individual coaching in person or online. She works with those who are struggling with separation and divorce and want a clear plan to navigate through the process.
www.bridgetobliss.com

Vivienne Smith provides support, practical advice and inspiration to single mothers through her book, coaching, seminars and webinars. Her experience as a single mum prompted her to write *The Single Mum's Survival Guide: How to Pick Up the Pieces and Build a Happy New Life*. She's successfully turned a negative and distressing experience into an opportunity to help others get through similar challenges.
www.thesinglemumssurvivalguide.com

BOOKS

Loving What Is by Byron Katie

This is a book that changes lives. Byron Katie gets you to answer four questions about a relationship or situation you're unhappy with. Writing down the answers leads to a series of revelations. This book has single-handedly transformed my relationship with my mother and I have used the same concepts to strengthen my marriage. I use it time and again on challenging situations and people. Highly recommended.

The Five Love Languages by Gary Chapman

Gary explains how each of us expresses our love using one of five primary love languages: quality time, words of affirmation, gifts, acts of service and physical touch. If your language is different from that of your partner, your expressions of love might not be understood and appreciated. This has given me a greater understanding of the different ways in which my husband and I show love and how we want to receive it. Gary has also written *The Five Love Languages of Children*, which is another insightful read.

Work

WEBSITES

Sherry Bevan is a career confidence coach for women. Whether your confidence has dipped after a career break or redundancy or you're back at work and feel things could be better, Sherry will help you to get clear on what you really want, then find the way to go and do it. Her website is filled to the brim with specific resources to help you in the Work area of your life.

www.theconfidentmother.co.uk

Marie Forleo is my online business mentor. After following her video blogs, I went on to do her 'B-School' to get me fully to grips with setting up and running Project Me as an online business. Whether you're starting or growing your business or looking to make a big change in your personal life, Marie will help you reach the highest levels of your creative potential.

www.marieforleo.com

Holly & Co is an online hub that supports and inspires small creative businesses. Whether you're a jewellery maker, florist, illustrator or any other kind of Artisan looking for a way to make your business dreams take flight, they will support you on your unique journey. Created by notonthehighstreet.com founder Holly Tucker MBE, you'll find inspiration to make a living doing what you love.

www.holly.co

Mum and Working is a UK-based website that lists a range of flexible business opportunities, plus advice and support for working mothers. Sign up to their newsletter to get their weekly email of new job vacancies.

www.mumandworking.co.uk

Gingerbread provides expert advice and practical support, and campaigns for single parents to get back into the workforce.

www.gingerbread.org.uk

Do-it helps you find volunteer work that suits your personality and schedule. Enter your postcode to access their database of opportunities in your area, or you can search for volunteer jobs within specific organisations you'd like to support.

www.do-it.org

BOOKS

Playing Big: Find Your Voice, Your Mission, Your Message by Tara Mohr

Tara provides real, practical tools to help women identify their callings, unhook from praise and criticism, unlearn counterproductive 'good girl' habits, and begin taking bold action. If your big dreams feel stuck behind a wall of fear and self-doubt, complete the exercises in this book and start playing BIG!

The Millionaire Messenger by Brendon Burchard

This was a game-changing book for me and inspired me to package up my own life experiences and knowledge to help others to succeed. It's a simple ten-step plan for making an impact and an income with what you know.

Founded After 40: How to Start a Business When You Haven't Got Time to Waste by Glenda Shawley

This books leads you through the challenges of setting up a locally based business one step at a time. It has an accompanying downloadable workbook to help you get your new business off the ground successfully.

BUSINESS MASTERMINDS AND MEET-UPS

DrivenWoman is a women's LifeWorking™ network where like-minded women support each other to achieve their goals. With monthly in-person meet-ups, you'll find the camaraderie and support of women who are pursuing their dreams, while keeping a close eye on their work–life balance. DrivenWoman meet-ups happen in person, in more and more locations around the world. Check the website for a meet-up near you. www.drivenwoman.co.uk

Mpower is a virtual and in-person mastermind and business support community offering practical and emotional support for mothers running their own business. Part of the magic of being part of Mpower is the inspiration, insights and energy you get from being surrounded by the right people. You gain access to experts and a community of other businesswomen with a wealth of personal experience, to get your questions answered and take steps with confidence.
www.mpower.global

Fun and Friendships

BOOKS

Friendships Don't Just Happen by Shasta Nelson

This book reveals the significant role our friendships play in our happiness and fulfilment. It's full of practical tips, fun activities, guided questions and step-by-step instructions to help you make new friends and enhance your relationships with your existing ones. Shasta's follow-up book *Frientimacy* explores the most common complaints and conflicts facing female friendships today, and lays out strategies for overcoming these pitfalls to create deeper, supportive relationships that last for the long term.

The Project Me Power Pal Pack

I created this guide and workbook to help you join forces with friends, to motivate and hold each other accountable towards your goals so you can work on your Project Me together. It contains everything you need to create meaningful meet-ups that'll make a valuable difference to all areas of your life.

www.myprojectme.com

COURSES

Project Me online courses/workshops/retreats

Join a Project Me online course for step-by-step guidance in your 8 Key Life Areas. With fun and easy-to-follow videos and worksheets, you'll take your Project Me to a whole new level. To find out about online courses, live workshops and retreats, join the newsletter list at www.myprojectme.com.

Udemy offer a huge range of online courses that can be done from the comfort of home and work around family commitments. They have everything from photography, nutrition, complementary therapies, business courses, writing, fashion design, floristry, sign language, virtual assistant training, Photoshop, learning musical instruments . . . you get the picture! www.udemy.com

WEBSITES

MumsMeetUp is a unique web-based app which connects mums locally and across the UK, enabling them to find mums like themselves in their area and playmates for their children. If you're a single mother, or you work full-time, or you want a running buddy, or you have a child with a disability, you'll have more of a chance of meeting a mother with similar interests and circumstances straight away.

www.mumsmeetup.com

16 Personalities Test

Take this free online test to discover your personality type, to learn more about yourself and others. You'll get a freakishly accurate description of who you are and why you do things the way you do.

www.16personalities.com

TED Talk by Susan Cain: The Power of Introverts

If you take the personality test above and fall on the introvert end of the spectrum, or you think your child does, it's well worth watching this hugely popular TED Talk. Susan's book *Quiet* and website The Quiet Revolution inspire all personality types to rethink what 'quiet' means.

www.quietrev.com

PODCAST

Happier with Gretchen Rubin

Co-hosted by *The Happiness Project* author Gretchen Rubin and her dry-witted sister Elizabeth Craft, this podcast gives you thought-provoking, practical advice about happiness hacks and good habits. The banter between the two sisters makes it a fun and easy listen.

www.gretchenrubin.com/podcast

Money

WEBSITES

Julie Feuerborn (aka 'Julie The Money Coach') offers individual coaching as well as online courses to help you review your finances and get unstuck. She offers caring step-by-step guidance to set up an easy-to-manage financial planning system to reach your long-term goals.

www.juliethemoneycoach.com

Denise Duffield-Thomas is a money mindset mentor who helps women release their fear of money, get paid what they're worth and take back control over their finances. If you're a working mother, particularly if you're running your own business, Denise's website is filled with helpful blog posts and free online workshops to help you move past your money blocks.

www.denisedt.com

Couple Money is a website that helps couples work out solutions that address their needs. They tackle some common money situations that couples have to deal with and their podcast includes how to talk to kids about money and instil good money ethics. www.couplemoney.com

Suddenly Single Money offers emotional and financial help after a bereavement, divorce or separation. Using neuro-linguistic programming, counselling and other techniques, they help to empower and enable you to work through your issues and move forward to the next phase of your life. www.suddenlysinglemoney.com

The Institute of Professional Willwriters helps you understand how to choose someone to make your will, the different ways of making a will, your options for keeping your will safe and much more. They'll also help you find a member of the institute local to you so you can reach out and get the process moving. www.ipw.org.uk

PODCAST

Her Money Matters is a podcast by money coach Jen Hemphill, who helps women organise their money in a simple, non-overwhelming way. She's a great source of information for women who want to get a handle on spending and saving. www.jenhemphill.com

APPS

Money Dashboard is an app that allows you to link your various bank and credit card accounts into one place, to make managing your money easier. It shows you exactly where your money goes to help you make better decisions. www.moneydashboard.com

The Secret to Money app is based on Rhonda Byrne's book *The Secret*. It's a fun personal-development programme of daily activities, featuring powerful practices that will help you develop a wealth mindset. You begin by listing seven things you'd buy if money were no object, then you deposit an imaginary amount of money into an account each day. There are daily affirmations and reminders to stay focused on your desires so you can manifest them faster.

Acknowledgements

I'm deeply grateful to the chain of incredible people involved in the journey of creating this book. Starting, of course, with my mother, 'Vagabond Ginger', for bringing me into the world. It wasn't easy and now that I'm a mother myself, I get it. To my best friend and husband Luca *(turn a different corner and we never would have met)*, and our amazing boys Max and Marco. Your love and support mean more to me than anything else in the world. How could I have written about overcoming so many challenges if you'd not challenged me so much? You're my most treasured teachers and I love you to infinity and beyond.

Elaine and the Parent Practice team threw me a lifeline when my family life was spiralling out of control. They led me to life coach Frances King who got me to think, 'Enough about the kids – what about ME?' This kick-started the monthly 'ASK' sessions with my Power Pals, Anna and Suzie – and the concept of Project Me was born. I'm immensely grateful to have you two utterly fabulous women in my life, always learning and growing together.

Ylwa, thank you for giving me my own motivational column which sparked the idea for my blog. The wonderful Nathalie and Kiki then hooked me up with Elizabeth Sheinkman of WME who said, 'There's a book in this . . .' and went on to become my agent. Elizabeth, thank you for your faith in my concept and your top-notch connections that led me to Amanda Harris, my commissioning editor at Orion Spring. Thank you Amanda, Olivia and the team at Orion for shaping this dream into reality.

My gratitude list also includes Basia for easing me out of thinking I have to design everything myself (and for doing such a beautiful job), Celine for giving me a tranquil (and gorgeous) writing space for a few days when I needed it most, and Leonor for your always helpful and dedicated research, assistance and friendship.

It's with thanks to all of my dear friends, near and far, that I score highly in the Fun and Friendships area of my life each month. Friends truly are the sunshine of life.

A special thanks to all of the mothers who've shared their stories for this book. You prove that we're not alone in our struggles. I appreciate and admire your authenticity and vulnerability. Continue to stay true to yourself. One small step at a time will get you to wherever you want to be.

A big shout-out to my Project Me Goal Diggers. Thank you for trusting me to guide you towards reaching your goals. Your accomplishments become my own success stories and I continue to feel so proud of you. Keep going – you've got this! I send you all love and gratitude. *(For I learn so much from you too.)*

To all mothers everywhere who are a part of the global Project Me tribe. A portion of proceeds from this book, online courses, workshops and retreats goes to charities that support vulnerable mothers. Mothers supporting mothers – we're all in this together.

About the Author

Kelly Pietrangeli is the *Mama Motivator* behind www.myprojectme.com, inspiring mothers to find a happier balance by looking closely at what is and what isn't working well in their lives. Her tools and resources make it easy to take small steps that lead to big results.

Kelly walks her talk. She's candid about her struggles and openly shares what has and hasn't worked in all areas of her life. Her ongoing quest for personal and professional growth is an inspiration to all that follow her popular blog, read her guest publications, attend her workshops and retreats and participate in her online programmes.

She's not afraid to kick you up the backside if you need it, but her style is gentle and encouraging, never brash or bossy. She inspires without intimidating, always encouraging a 'be easier on your yourself' approach with plenty of permission to 'drop the guilt'.

She considers the different stages mothers are at in their journey, and gives permission to take baby steps, at your own pace, creating self-devised, not pre-prescribed, action plans.

Kelly lives in London with her husband and their two teenage boys.